Report on Constitutional Enforcement and Constitutional Review in China

Li Lin, Zhai Guoqiang

Paths International Ltd

中国社会科学出版社
CHINA SOCIAL SCIENCES PRESS

Abstract: Judicial review of constitutionality is not regarded as the basic method for enforcing the Constitution in China, which is different from the Western countries. According to the Constitution, the Standing Committee of the National People's Congress has the authority to interpret the constitution and review the constitutionality of the legal system. However, there is neither an effective constitutional interpretation nor constitutional decision made by the authority. In China, the Constitution mainly acts as a political guide or declaration and it is enforced by political means instead of legal means. However, in order to build the rule of law, the constitution has also been enforced as a legal norm in the past thirty years.

This report analyzes the operating mechanism of the implementation of the constitution and the constitutional review system in China. From the perspective of comparative law, the implementation of the mechanism of constitutional review in China should not copy the experience in Western countries, and the relevant departments and State organs should be comprehensively integrated in order to advance the supervision of the implementation of the constitution. This report also suggests the establishment of a Constitutional Council mechanism inside the NPC system.

Key words: Implementation of the Constitution, Constitutional Review, Constitutional Council, NPC system

Contents

A constitution is the fundamental law of a country. The implementation of a constitution is the primary task for carrying out the rule of law and building a country under the rule of law. Relative to the establishment of a constitution, the implementation of a constitution involves how to turn the text of a constitution into a set of practical theories, systems and mechanisms.① In China's constitutional history, both constitution establishment (constitutionalism) and constitution implementation actually embody a "line of thought for changing the legal system" — establishing and implementing a constitution to change the current situation of institutional operations and shape a new constitutional order. Hence, the importance of implementing a constitution is emphasized at the time of establishing a constitution, whether during the activities regarding the establishment of the constitution since the founding of the new China or in the events for the establishment of the constitution during the period of the Republic of China.② Therefore, constitution implementation is always an important topic in theoretical research on the constitution in China.

Guaranteeing constitution implementation is the fundamental requirement for ensuring the will and interests of the people across the country, and maintaining prolonged stability of the Party and the country. It is also the fundamental requirement for building a moderately

① Cai Dingjian, "the Concept of Constitution Implementation and the Way to Implement the Constitution", *China Legal Science*, 2004 (1).

② After the adoption of the current constitution, Chinese politicians made explanatory notes for the draft constitution, delivered public speeches and adopted other means to stress the importance of the implementation of the constitution. After the establishment of the constitution in 1954, Mao Zedong specially emphasized, "The Constitution must be implemented, and failure to do so amounts to violation of the Constitution." In the period of the Republic of China, the constitutional convention of Zhejiang Province adopted the *Law of Zhejiang Province on Constitution Implementation* through a resolution along with the establishment of a provincial constitution. According to the explanation from scholars at that time, a constitution was not inherent in the old system, thus it was necessary to repeal the old constitution and establish a new one, and implement a constitution based on the old system. A similar constitutional document is the *Preparatory Procedure for Constitution Implementation* adopted in the National Assembly in 1946. See Xia Xinhua et al., *The Constitutional Course in Modern China: A Gathering of Historical Materials*, China University of Political Science and Law Press, 2004, p.708.

prosperous society in all aspects, comprehensively intensifying the reform, practicing law-based governance of the country and strengthening party self-discipline in an all-round way. It serves as the fundamental guarantee for national prosperity, the people's happiness and the realization of the Chinese dream for the great rejuvenation of the Chinese nation.

As early as June 14, 1954, when delivering a speech entitled *On the Draft Constitution of the People's Republic of China* in the 30th Session of the Central People's Government Committee, Mao Zedong stressed, "After the adoption of the draft constitution, everyone across the country should implement it; in particular, state personnel should take the lead in such implementation, those present in this session should implement it first. Failure to implement it constitutes violation of it."

On November 26, 1982, when he delivered the *Report on the Draft Amendment to the Constitution of the People's Republic of China* during the 5th Session of the 5th National People's Congress, comrade Peng Zhen once again pointed out, "After deliberation and official adoption in this National People's Congress, the draft amendment to the Constitution will be implemented as the fundamental law of the State with the greatest authority and supreme legal authority. It will serve as the general constitution for administering State affairs well and ensuring national security in China during the new historical period. We believe that the new Constitution is bound to be strictly observed and implemented... the National People's Congress and its Standing Committee have the authority to supervise its implementation, while the local people's congresses at various levels shall ensure the observance and implementation of the Constitution within their administrative areas." When reporting in the 12th National Congress of the Communist Party of China, comrade Hu Yaobang proclaimed solemnly, "It is particularly necessary to educate and supervise Party members to take the lead in observing the Constitution and laws. As stipulated in the new Constitution of the Communist Party of China, the Party must conduct its activities within the framework of the Constitution and laws of the country; this is a vitally important principle. None of the activities of the Party organization and Party members from the central level to the grass-roots level must contravene the Constitution and laws of the country.

The Chinese people and the Communist Party of China have deeply understood that the authority of the Constitution has a vital bearing on the political stability and national destiny. We brook no damage to the constitutional foundation...the Communist Party of China has led the Chinese people to establish the new Constitution and will also join the people of all nationalities across the country, democratic parties and people's organizations to safeguard the sanctity of the Constitution and guarantee the implementation of the Constitution. After the adoption of the Constitution, it is essential to adopt various means for launching extensive publicity to make the Constitution widely known. One billion people should develop the concept and habit of abiding by and safeguarding the Constitution and should fight against the acts of violating and disrupting the Constitution; this is a great power."

On December 4, 2002, Hu Jintao delivered a speech during the meeting of the people from all walks of life in the Capital on celebrating the 20th anniversary of the promulgation and implementation of the Constitution of the People's Republic of China, he pointed out, "In order to carry out the basic strategy of law-based governance of the country, we must first implement the Constitution in an all-round way. In order to comprehensively implement it, we must improve the constitutional guarantee system to ensure the implementation of the Constitution. Twenty years have witnessed continuous improvement in the implementation of China's Constitution, and acting in accordance with the Constitution and laws is becoming a common code of conduct in the society. However, it should also be noted that under the new situation of developing a socialist market economy, as laws and systems are underdeveloped and the quality of law enforcement personnel do not fully adapt to such a situation, there are many problems regarding the failure to abide by laws, strictly enforce laws and punish law-breakers, and some cases of violating the Constitution to varying degrees still exist. It is imperative to study and improve the mechanism for the supervision of the constitution, further clarify the constitutional supervision procedure so that all acts which violate the Constitution can be opportunely corrected. The National People's Congress and its Standing Committee shall proceed from the fundamental interests of the state and the people to fully guarantee the freedom and rights of the citizens as prescribed by the

Constitution during legislation; practically assume the responsibility for supervising the implementation of the Constitution, resolutely redress the unconstitutional acts; faithfully perform the function of interpreting the Constitution, and make necessary explanations about the issues during the implementation of the Constitution so as to better implement it. The local people's congresses at various levels and their standing committees shall earnestly ensure that the Constitution is observed and implemented in their administrative areas. The state administrative, adjudication and procuratorial organs at various levels shall uncompromisingly carry out the Constitution, conduct administration according to laws, maintain judicial justice, and continuously enhance the quality of law enforcement personnel, and their ability to enforce laws. No organization or individual has the privilege of going above the Constitution and laws."

On December 4, 2012, when speaking during the meeting of the people from all walks of life in the Capital on celebrating the 30th anniversary of the promulgation and implementation of the current constitution, Xi Jinping pointed out, "The 30-year course of its development fully proves that China's Constitution is a good constitution, consistent with national conditions, the reality and the developmental requirements of the era; it is a good constitution which fully reflects the common will of the people, fully guarantees the democratic rights of the people, and adequately safeguards the fundamental interests of the people; it is a good constitution which promotes national development and progress, and ensures that the people can create a happy life and that the Chinese nation can achieve great rejuvenation; it serves as the fundamental legal guarantee for China and the people to withstand various difficulties and risks, and always follow the socialist road with Chinese characteristics towards advancement…we can clearly realize that the Constitution is closely linked to the country's future and the people's destiny…guaranteeing the implementation of the Constitution ensures that the realization of the fundamental interests of the people. As long as we earnestly respect and effectively implement the Constitution, there is a guarantee that the people are the masters of the country and the cause of the Party and the country can develop smoothly. On the contrary, if the Constitution is ignored, weakened, even destroyed, the people's freedom and rights cannot be guaranteed, and the cause of the Party and the country will suffer setbacks...in parallel with fully recognizing the achievements, we should also be aware of the drawbacks, which mainly includes: the supervisory mechanism and specific systems for guaranteeing the implementation of the Constitution are still underdeveloped, and failure to abide by laws, strictly enforce laws and punish law-breakers still exists in some areas and departments; the law enforcement and judicial problems having a bearing on the immediate interests of the people are still relatively striking; some public servants abuse power, commit dereliction and breach of duty, break laws in law enforcement, and even bend the law for personal gain, severely damaging the authority of the national legal system; the constitutional awareness of citizens including some leading cadres needs to be further enhanced. We must attach great importance to these problems and solve them practically."

The Third Plenary Session of the 18th Central Committee of the Communist Party of China once again explicitly vowed to comprehensively implement the Constitution. The *Decision of the Central Committee of the Communist Party of China on Some Major Issues Concerning Comprehensively Promoting Law-based Governance of the Country*, adopted in the Fourth Plenary Session of the 18th Central Committee of the Communist Party of China, specifies further arrangements for implementing the Constitution. The Decision covers seven parts — the second part focuses on improving the socialist legal system with Chinese characteristics with the Constitution as the core, and strengthening the implementation of the Constitution, with top priority given to improving the system for the supervision over the implementation of the constitution. Reinforcing supervision over the implementation of the Constitution is an important measure decided by the Fourth Plenary Session of the 18th Central Committee of the Communist Party of China.

1. Basic Situation of the Implementation of China's Constitution

As we know, the Constitution is highly political. The overall implementation of China's Constitution shows that the Ruling Party always regards the Constitution as a paramount political and legal document. Attaching importance to the political guarantee for the implementation of the Constitution is an important characteristic of the implementation of the Constitution in China. In the opinions of relevant leaders involved in drafting the Constitution, on the one hand, the implementation of the Constitution should rely on the leadership of the Ruling Party; on the other hand, all forces should be mobilized to ensure the implementation of the Constitution in various respects. Furthermore, we should rely on the power of the masses to guarantee the implementation of the Constitution. This is a political path towards implementation with the hope of realizing the political goals enshrined in the Constitution by changing the concept of the general public regarding the Constitution before influencing their behavior. In the *Report on the Draft Amendment to the Constitution of the People's Republic of China*, Peng Zhen, one of the main founders of China' socialist legal system, pointed out that "one billion of people should develop the concept and habit of abiding by and safeguarding the Constitution and should fight against the acts of violating and disrupting the Constitution; this is a great power". Therefore, enhancing the concept and awareness of the people regarding the Constitution is of particular significance in the political implementation of China's Constitution. This is exactly the purpose of the establishment of the National Constitution Day and the system of pledging allegiance to the Constitution as put forward in the Fourth Plenary Session of the 18th Central Committee of the Communist Party of China! These measures are conducive to improving the concept and awareness of the people from all sectors of society regarding the Constitution, and stimulating "the people of all nationalities, all state organs and armed forces, various parties and social organizations, enterprises and public organizations across China" to actively base their activities on the Constitution, carry out their activities within the scope of the Constitution, guarantee the implementation of the Constitution and safeguard the authority of the Constitution.

According to the study of comparative constitutions, most of the Western countries under the rule of law have a special law-based implementation organ. There is merely a political implementation mechanism and no law-based implementation mechanism only in a few constitutional modes.[①] Therefore, mainstream Western constitutional theory emphasizes a law-based implementation of the Constitution and holds that the judicial organ enjoys an advantageous position in implementing the Constitution.[②] Of course, the judicature is not the only way for implementing the Constitution, since the political department can also implement the Constitution.[③] The political implementation and law-based implementation of the Constitution in Western countries can be broadly summarized as follows: the legal organ only deals with legal matters, while the political matters are addressed by the political organ.

As a special form of written constitution, China's Constitution has

---

① Thomas C.Grey, "Constitutionalism: An Analytic Framework", in Richard N. Bronaugh, Michael A. Eizenga, Stephen B. Sharzer (eds.), Readings in the Philosophy of Constitutional Law, Kendall/Hunt Publishing Company, January 1992.

② Norman Dorsen, Michel Rosenfeld, Andras Sajo, Susanne Baer, "Comparative Constitutionalism: Cases and Materials", West Group (2003), p.109. Some scholars believe that judicial implementation may lead to excessive specialization of the Constitution and thus be divorced from the ordinary people. Stephen M. Griffin, "American Constitutionalism: From Theory to Politics", Princeton University Press, 1996, pp.16-17.

③ Stephen M. Griffin, "American Constitutionalism: From Theory to Politics", Princeton University Press, 1996, p.207.

both political and legal attributes.[①] However, unlike the constitutional implementation mode in Western countries, it is very difficult to distinguish political implementation of the Constitution from its law-based implementation in China by the work the organs undertake. Functionally, the legal organ may also participate in the political implementation of the Constitution, while the political organ may also engage in law-based implementation of the Constitution — with respect to the former, for example, the judicial organ carries out political learning and implementation activities concerning the Constitution;[②] with regard to the latter, for example, the Ruling Party reviews the compliance of the Party's system of rules and regulations with the Constitution (laws).[③] Actually, China's legal organ is not a pure legal department in most cases; instead, it is also a political department and performs certain political functions.

1.1 Political Path for Implementing China's Constitution

As a socialist constitution, China's Constitution inherits the basic institutional mode of the Soviet Union's Constitution and incorporates the institutional design based on the constitutional theory of Marxism.[④] This critical constitutional theory focuses on great social changes, while laws and regulations are only small cells in the social structure. Methodologically, the legal theory of Marxism addressed the constitution

---

① Some scholars believed China's Constitution contained political clauses and legal clauses, which were implemented in different ways, see Zhang Qianfan, On Selection and Application of the Constitution, *Peking University Law Journal*, 2012 (5); Xue Xiaojian, Legal Cornerstone for China's Social Transformation: The Historical Status of the Constitution Revised in 1982, *China Legal Science*, 2012 (4).

② See the circular of the Supreme People's Court about learning and implementing the *Amendments to the Constitution of the People's Republic of China*, the circular of the Supreme People's Procuratorate about earnestly implementing the *Circular of the Central Committee of the Communist Party of China Concerning Further Learning and Implementing the Constitution of the People's Republic of China.*

③ See the *Regulations for Making the Rules and Regulations of the Communist Party of China and the Regulations for Filing of the Rules*, and the *Regulations and Normative Documents of the Communist Party of China.*

④ William C. Jones, "The Constitution of the People's Republic of China", 63 Wash. U. L. Q. 707, 1985.

from the perspective of the sociology of law and took the constitution as a political form.[①] Afterwards, the Soviet Union's theory of national law excessively stressed that the constitution mirrored the realistic power relationship, and overlooked the function of the constitution as law in regulating political relationships. Under the influence of the above philosophies and systems, the Constitution of China that is currently in force contains many clauses which confirm the political goals.[②] For example, the preamble to the Constitution identifies the basic tasks and basic lines of the State, and the general principles of the Constitution stipulate various programmatic and policy clauses.[③] From the perspective of comparative law, China's Constitution seems more like a declaration that is similar to a political program and relies more on political implementation.[④] In political implementation, the political goals are higher than laws and regulations. Accordingly, this mode of implementation does not differentiate various level of legal effects, and treats the Constitution and general laws equally, even insists

① (Austria) Hans Kelsen, "The Legal Theory of Communism", trans. by Wang Mingyang, China Legal Publishing House, 2004, pp.238-239.

② Therefore, some scholars criticized that China's constitutional clauses were too vague so that there was a lack of an effective implementation mechanism (see Tony Saich, The Fourth Constitution of the People's Republic of China, 9 Rev. Socialist L. 113, p.122 (1983)); for criticism and reflection on this point of view, see Janet E. Ainsworth, "Interpreting Sacred Texts: Preliminary Reflections on Constitutional Discourse in China", 43 *Hastings Law Journal*, p.273, 297 (1992).

③ Some Western scholars believed that with the dual influence of the Confucian cultural tradition and the socialist tradition, many clauses in China's Constitution are kinds of goal-oriented clauses. See Janet E. Ainsworth, "Interpreting Sacred Texts: Preliminary Reflections on Constitutional Discourse in China", 43 *Hastings Law Journal*, p.273, 297 (1992); Teemu Ruskola, "Legal Orientalism", 101 *Michigan Law Review* 179 (2002).

④ Guo Danqing even believed that China's Constitution was similar to the United States Declaration of Independence — although it was important, it actually had no legal binding effect (see Donald C. Clarke, "Puzzling Observations in Chinese Law: When Is a Riddle Just a Mistake?", in C. Stephen Hsu (ed.), Understanding China's Legal System, New York: New York University Press, 2003, p.106). Chen Duanhong held that the implementation of China's Constitution was mainly "political implementation" by the Communist Party of China and the government, thus judicial implementation was excluded (see Chen Duanhong, The Power to Make the Constitution and the Fundamental Law, China Democracy and Law Press, 2010, p.279).

that it is equivalent to rules and regulations; it only serves as a carrier for confirming goals. Therefore, in China's political discourse, the implementation of the Constitution is often accompanied by amendments to the Constitution, and both processes with totally different operational logic become an "organic unity" in political implementation — both are designed to realize or carry out a certain political goal. Thus it is a practice, in China's constitutional development, that constitutional implementation is promoted in a political way following an amendment to the Constitution.

Under the rigid institutional mode of the constitution, the realization of political goals depends upon the Constitution, and different political subjects interpret and further develop the normative definitions in the Constitution to respond to social changes and achieve the political goals.[①] Although the rigid amendment procedure is set in form in China's Constitution, it is closer to a flexible constitution in practical operation. As shown by the facts concerning previous amendments to the Constitution, social changes are reflected in China's Constitution by amending the Constitution rather than by interpreting it.

Under the flexible institutional mode of the constitution, previous amendments to the Constitution were intended more to constitutionalize the political goals, and integrate the political goals with the Constitution to promote constitutional implementation and achieve the political goals. In this process, the Ruling Party has always assumed the heavy responsibility for discovering and confirming fundamental norms[②] — cognizing the changes in social values and concepts — moderately adjusting the political goals — initiating the constitutional amendment

① Keith E. Whittington, "Constitutional Construction: Divided Powers and Constitutional Meaning", Harvard University Press, 1999, p.207.

② One important function of the Communist Party of China lies in making an organizational expression of social will and attempting to build connections between the State and the society. See Susan L. Shirk, "The Chinese Political System and the Political Strategy of Economic Reform", in Kenneth G. Lieberthal & David M. Lampton (eds.), Bureaucracy, Politics, and Decision Making in Post-Mao China, University Of California Press, 1992; Similar opinions refer to Larry Cata Backer, "Party, People, Government and State: On Constitutional Values and the Legitimacy of The Chinese State-Party Rule of Law System", 331 *Boston University International Law Journal*, 2012, pp.30-47.

procedure to enable constitutionalization. This constitutional amendment is also called "confirmative constitutional amendment mode" by some scholars. From this perspective, the Constitution is only a segment in a greater political system, and constitutional implementation is a means for realizing the political goals. In the political system, it is necessary to implement not only the regulations of the Constitution but also political value concepts and norms such as the political goals, the Party's constitution and disciplines. The path of political implementation lies in making overall arrangements by placing the Constitution under a longer historical dimension and a more macroscopic social background — the Constitution is carried out by attaching it to achievement of the political goals, thus some scholars consider it as "affiliated constitutional implementation", in which the Constitution is deemed more as a political form and must be advanced with political development. In political practice, the Constitution is often implemented by extensive political mobilization led by the Ruling Party. Its main characteristics are as follows:

First, the Party organizations at various levels play the leading role.[①] As shown by the history of the establishment of a constitution, this is also the plan for the establishment of a constitution designed by constitution makers. According to the political philosophy at the time of the establishment of the constitution, the implementation of the Constitution relies on the Party's leadership and on the people[②] — political mobilization is conducted by the organizational force of the Communist Party of China and high organizational capability of the Party organizations at various levels. Unlike the general political parties, the Communist Party of China plays the core role in China's political system, with its organizational forces available in state organs, people's organizations, enterprises and public institutions, mass organizations, even in

---

① In this regard, in the opinion of Peng Zhen, former top legislator, the Constitution is implemented mainly by relying on state organs, especially the organizations of the Communist Party of China. See Peng Zhen, Further Implementing the Constitution, Acting in Strict Compliance with the Constitution, *China Legal Science*, 1984 (1).

② Wang Hanbin, "Interviews with Wang Hanbin — Experiencing Socialist Democracy and Building of the Legal System in the New Period", China Democracy and Law Press, 2012, p.128.

non-public economic organizations. From the perspective of functionalism, the Communist Party of China serves as the bond among different subsystems in Chinese society, and has theories, systems, organizations and personnel in different fields. Furthermore, the Communist Party of China has a high capability of mobilization for allocating various resources and has set up organizations in different systems, thus laying a foundation for political implementation of the Constitution.①

Second, the main forces for implementing the Constitution during political mobilization are available in a wide scope, while all state organs including legal organs, social groups and social organizations are among these forces.② Under the political mobilization mode, the forces for guaranteeing the implementation of the Constitution are increasingly socialized, even the common people are also among the main forces for implementing the Constitution.③ Under the above mobilization system, democratic parties also form an important part of the system for political

① This kind of political mobilization mode dates back to the mass movement mode adopted by the Communist Party of China when it seized and consolidated political power in the early period — it first identified a short-term goal and then mobilized the political system to move toward that goal, ultimately extended to the common people. See Doak A. Barnett, Cadres, Bureaucracy, and Political Power in Communist China, New York: Columbia University Press, 1967, pp.437-438.

② In this respect, Hu Sheng, former head of the Working Group of the Central Committee of the Communist Party of China for the Constitution once stated, "The implementation of the Constitution is guaranteed by all state organs including the people's congresses, their standing committees, all judicial, procuratorial, administrative organs and the people across the country; this is a complete system for protecting the implementation of the Constitution." See Liu Zheng, The Historical Trace of the System of People's Congress, China Democracy and Law Press, 2008, p.236.

③ According to Peng Zhen's explanation, besides all state organs, the main forces for implementing the Constitution also include such social organizations as trade unions, the Women's Federation, the Communist Youth League and such grass-roots mass self-governing organizations as residents committees and villagers committees, and news and public opinion organizations including newspapers, magazines, radio and television, and all of the people. Such political mobilization relies on the strength of the people and makes the Constitution and laws become extremely familiar to the people, so it is necessary to value the publicity and education concerning the Constitution, develop the concept of safeguarding the Constitution and fight against the acts which violate the Constitution. See Peng Zhen, Speech in the First Session of the 6th National People's Congress, June 21, 1983.

mobilization. In China, the system of multi-party cooperation and political consultation at different levels serves as the main platform for mobilizing other political parties. According to the Constitution of the Chinese People's Political Consultative Conference, one important duty of the Chinese People's Political Consultative Conference is to exercise democratic supervision over the implementation of the Constitution. Such supervision is exercised by engaging with the people to learn about the implementation of the Constitution, and then putting forward the opinions for guaranteeing the implementation of the Constitution, and meanwhile publicizing the new Constitution among the people and educating the people to get familiar with, abide by and safeguard the Constitution.[①] In addition, the constitutions of most of the democratic parties provide that the party should conduct activities in accordance with the Constitution of the People's Republic of China, the fundamental standard, and should be responsible for safeguarding the sanctity of the Constitution and guaranteeing the implementation of the Constitution. [②]

Third, the fields for such political implementation are also very extensive. China's Constitution contains a large number of purpose articles, covering political, economic, social and cultural fields. Therefore, in a broad sense, the general national acts can be incorporated within the scope of the implementation of the constitution, and the developments and changes in the general pattern of the relationship of state power can also be considered as the implementation of the system of democratic centralism prescribed by the Constitution or the implementation of the articles concerning central and local relationships. According to the Constitution, even the family planning, forest planting, mandarin popularization and other activities carried out by state organs can be deemed as acts of implementation of the constitution.

① Zhang Youyu, "Constitutionalism Review (II)", Masses Press, 1986, p.341.

② For example, the *Constitution of the Chinese Peasants' and Workers' Democratic Party* provides that the party should conduct activities in accordance with the Constitution of the People's Republic of China as the fundamental standard, and should be responsible for safeguarding the sanctity of the Constitution and guaranteeing its implementation.The party enjoys political freedom, organizational independence and equal legal status within the scope of the rights and obligations prescribed by the Constitution. There are similar stipulations in the constitutions of other democratic parties.

Fourth, specific ways for such political implementation include meetings, notices and resolutions concerning implementation of the Constitution. In China's political operation, a meeting is an important way for realizing political goals since it is convened to form resolutions to be executed, or a meeting is held to solicit opinions, release signals and show attitudes. The higher the level of the meeting is, the more important the meeting is — it is supposed to make organizations at various levels realize its significance, and a meeting's decision is implemented from top to bottom on a level-by-level basis; for example, after the revision of the constitution, the Political Bureau of the Central Committee of the Communist Party of China held a special meeting to study and arrange for the implementation of the Constitution. Moreover, in order to enhance the constitutional awareness, state organs at various levels also held commemorations to publicize and carry out the Constitution. Besides meetings, the ways for political promotion of the implementation of the constitution also include political resolutions, notices or instructions and speeches.① For example, the Central Committee of the Communist Party of China issued documents requiring various departments, especially political and legal departments, to actively and systematically check whether there is any form of noncompliance with the Constitution in work, and lose no time in earnestly correcting such noncompliance (if any).② In response to this, the Party organizations in various areas and departments carried out top-down mobilization, and activities for learning about and implementing the Constitution. In order to ensure the effect of such mobilization on implementation, the mechanisms of guarantee including evaluation, examination, comparison, and reward may be attached.

In general, the political implementation of China's Constitution features a mobilization mode led by the governing party — forces are concentrated within a specific temporal and spatial scope to handle special affairs in a special way. Such political implementation of the

① Wu Guoguang called this way Documentary Politics, and said that these political documents were often not officially promulgated before repeated solicitation of opinions from various parties, revision and improvement. See Yu Keping, Li Kanru, China's Political Development, Social Sciences Academic Press, 2013, pp.323-324.

② Liu Zheng, "The Historical Trace of the System of the People's Congress", China Democracy and Law Press, 2008, pp.149-150.

Constitution is the product of a highly political society in china. Before reform and the opening-up, resources were highly concentrated in the whole country and society, and all social subsystems were subordinate to or absorbed by the political system.① Accordingly, the independence and self-sufficiency of the legal system are relatively weak, and its operation is characterized by attachment and subordination to the legal system, thus the so-called "party and government unification" system took shape. An important reform measure since the implementation of the constitution in 1982 is "separation of the Party's functions from those of the government". In fact, "government functions" include the formal legal system and routine governance conducted by administrative and judicial organs according to laws. Under the principle of separation of the Party's functions from those of the government, the functions and powers of the Party organizations are mainly restricted to some basic and important matters, while the relatively specific management is exercised according to the routine systems. Susan L. Shirk called this governance mode "management by exception"② — the governing party focuses on handling major matters which can not be addressed through routine governance, in which case, once an agreement is reached, they are addressed through routine governance. The political implementation of the Constitution is promoted mainly by the highest political authority and reflects a mode of "management by exception". This mode can mobilize various forces in a short period of time, but a routine law enforcement mechanism is necessary to develop a long-term mechanism for promoting the implementation of the constitution.

1.2 Legal Mechanism for Implementing China's Constitution

As mentioned above, the political implementation of the Constitution

① Sociology scholars generally call it a "totalistic society", see Sun Liping, Wang Hansheng, Wang Sibin et al., Changes in China's Social S tructure since Reform, *Social Sciences in China*, 1994 (2).

② Susan L. Shirk, "The Chinese Political System and the Political Strategy of Economic Reform", in Kenneth G. Lieberthal & David M. Lampton (eds.), Bureaucracy, Politics, and Decision Making in Post-Mao China, University of California Press, 1992.

is a non-routine "management by exception" mode, while law enforcement features a routine governance mode. If the political implementation is considered to emphasize dynamic changes and trying to change a status quo through the implementation of the constitution, the law enforcement stresses stability and maintenance of the existing constitutional order. In China, an important precondition for this law enforcement mechanism is that the legal system must be gradually separated from the political system and become a relatively independent operational mechanism different from the political system. Against such a background, the Constitution performs the function of a legal norm, and state organs deem the Constitution as a binding legal norm, and implement the Constitution in the legislation, judicial and administrative process. Under the operational mechanism for law enforcement, the implementation of the Constitution is broadly classified into two categories — passive implementation and active implementation of the constitution. The former takes the Constitution as a boundary — state organs observe the Constitution and shall not violate the Constitution, so realization is mainly based on control over compliance with the Constitution, while the latter means that state organs actively regard the Constitution as the basis for actions, and a legal order for constitutional compliance is achieved, which includes: constitutional norms and instructions are realized according to procedural norms and substantive norms of the Constitution.

1.2.1 Passive implementation of the constitution

Under the mechanism of passive implementation of the constitution, all state acts should not go beyond the boundary of the Constitution, and the legal norm system and state acts are controlled in terms of constitutional compliance by means of a certain procedural and institutional design.[①] Generally, passive implementation of the

① Zhang Qianfan called it substantive implementation — state acts are controlled for constitutional compliance according to the Constitution as the standard. See Zhang Qianfan, Concept and Path of Constitution Implementation, *Tsinghua Law Review*, 2012 (6).

constitution mainly features constitutional compliance control exercised by a constitutional review body such as a judicial organ or a constitutional court or constitutional committee. However, whether decentralization mode or a centralization mode is adopted, the control mechanism for constitutional compliance presents the characteristic of being unique for the ease of safeguarding the unity of the entire legal system. In China, there is no powerful legal body to conduct constitutional review. China's Constitution and Legislation Law provide that the National People's Congress and its Standing Committee should exercise constitutional supervision and correct the unconstitutional acts, but the organ of power has not yet made a legally valid decision. Therefore, constitutional theory mostly holds that China lacks a substantive constitutional review system. If the constitutional review system upholds that the Constitution is interpreted and constitutional judgment is made by a special constitutional review body, there is no centralized constitutional review in China. However, China does not lack a control mechanism for constitutional compliance with the Constitution as the legal norm. In legal practice, state organs correct the unconstitutional acts within the scope of their functions and powers, resulting in decentralized, diverse constitutional compliance control.

Generally, the typical case of passive implementation of the constitution is the judicial constitutional review mechanism. However, with the impact of a political concept and a pattern of power division, China's judicial organ does not implement the Constitution by means of a constitutional review and also never makes a constitutional judgment about constitutional compliance or constitutional incompliance.[①] In general judicial concept and judicial practice, the Constitution is not considered as a legal norm directly related to judgment.[②] China's judicial organ exercises control over constitutional compliance in another way.

① This system is not unique in China, and a similar system is also adopted in Belgium, Netherlands' courts. See Randall Peerenboom, China's Long March toward Rule of Law, Cambridge University Press, 2002, pp.260-261.

② According to the sampling survey on judges in 15 provinces and municipalities nationwide as conducted by Deng Shibao, most of the judges believed that the Constitution was less related to judgment. Deng Shibao, An Empirical Analysis of the Constitutional Awareness of Contemporary Chinese Judges, *Jinan Journal*, 2011 (1).

In judgment practice, courts choose the applicable conflicting legal norms to exclude the legal norms which violate the superior law from the judgment norm system so as to exercise constitutional compliance control of the "judgment norm system".[①] Under the current judicial system, although courts can choose and apply legal norms, they cannot identify the validity of relevant normative legal documents.[②] Therefore, such validity of constitutional compliance control only exists in the field of judicial judgment; furthermore, there is no system as a precedent to use as support, so its effect is limited.

According to China's Constitution, the legislative body performs the function of passive control over constitutional compliance. Besides the National People's Congress, local people's congresses also have the authority of control over constitutional compliance.[③] This is the mechanism of control over constitutional compliance prescribed at the level of legal texts. However, the legislative body never makes an annulment or revocation decision with legal validity, so such a formal mechanism of control over constitutional compliance is generally in a "sleep state". However, there is an informal, relatively routine mechanism

---

① According to *the Reply Letter Concerning Application of Laws and Administrative Regulations by the People's Courts in the Case of Noncompliance of Local Regulations and Provisions with Laws and Administrative Regulations in Hearing Administrative Cases, the Official Reply Concerning How the People's Courts Should Make Reference to Rules and Provisions without the Basis of Laws and Regulations in Hearing Administrative Cases, the Official Reply Concerning How the People's Courts Should Apply Laws in Hearing Administrative Cases Involving Road Transport*, etc, courts can refrain from applying the legal norms which conflict with the superior law. Kong Xiangjun, Selection and Application amid Legal Norm Conflicts and Filling of Loopholes, The People's Court Press, 2004, pp.212-213.

② Article 7 of the *Regulations of the Supreme People's Court Concerning Citation of Normative Legal Documents Including Laws and Regulations in Judgment Documents*; however, the consensus on whether conflicting with the superior law certainly leads to inapplicability has not yet been reached among different legal bodies. Commission of Legislative Affairs of the National People's Congress, Reply to the Legal Enquiries (2000-2005), China Democracy and Law Press, 2006, p.10.

③ For example, the *Interim Regulations of the Standing Committee of the People's Congress of Heilongjiang Province* explicitly provides that the standing committee of the people's congress is entitled to supervise the unconstitutional, law-breaking acts of a provincial people's government, provincial higher people's court, provincial people's procuratorate in exercising official powers.

of control over constitutional compliance within the people's congress systems at various levels. Under such an internal implementation mechanism, the Standing Committee of the National People's Congress deals with the legal norms which violate the Constitution and the superior law mainly by "opportunely strengthening communication and consultation with the legislative body, bringing forward opinions to urge it to revise or repeal them by itself."[①] A legal enquiry reply system has gradually taken shape in the legal practice of the Standing Committee of the National People's Congress. Article 55 of the Legislation Law also makes confirmation of such institutional practice at the legal level. According to this article, the working body of the Standing Committee of the National People's Congress can study and reply to specific legal matters. In this process, there was a large quantity of legal reasoning and decisions based on the Constitution and many disputes were settled in this internal communication and consultation.[②] Some legal matters involved how to understand the meaning of some parts of the text of the constitution and the constitutional compliance of public power acts; moreover, the legal working body of the people's congress interpreted constitution articles in some cases.[③] The mode under which the internal mechanism for the coordination of communications, including enquiry reply, is adopted in legal practice to make judgment about whether or not the disputed public power acts comply with or violate the Constitution is considered as an internal, informal constitutional

---

① Work Report of the Standing Committee of the National People's Congress, 2013.

② Commission of Legislative Affairs of the National People's Congress, Reply to the Legal Enquiries (2000-2005), China Democracy and Law Press, 2006, pp.168-169.

③ The constitutional interpretations in such internal operations do not appear in the form of constitutional interpretation, but they also become legally binding, such as interpretation of the scope of "administrative organs" prescribed by Article 89 of the Constitution, and the interpretation of the scope of protection of "Freedom and Privacy of Correspondence" prescribed by Article 40 of the Constitution. Separately, see Wang Hanbin, Interviews with Wang Hanbin — Experiencing Socialist Democracy and Building a Legal System in the New Period, China Democracy and Law Press, 2012, p.323; Commission of Legislative Affairs of the National People's Congress, Reply to the Legal Enquiries (2000-2005), China Democracy and Law Press, 2006, pp.129-130.

compliance control mode.[①]

During passive implementation of China's Constitution, administrative organs are also the important bodies for constitutional compliance control.[②] As the highest organ of state administration prescribed by the Constitution, the State Council will take the initiative to make decisions in some cases to correct noncompliance with the Constitution; for example, the State Council made judgments about the sales and leasing of the land owned by the collective and the state by local governments.[③] The State Council decided that the establishment of nationality towns by local governments violated the Constitution.[④] Furthermore, in China, the administrative organs even decide that some acts of judicial organs violate the Constitution, which is obviously different from the judicial constitutional review mode. For example, in the *Official Reply to Some Issues Concerning the People's Courts Requiring Post and Telecommunications Departments to Assist in Enforcement*

---

① For example, in reply, the Commission of Legislative Affairs of the National People's Congress believed that establishment of the standing committee by the township people's congress violated the Constitution. See Commission of Legislative Affairs of the National People's Congress, Reply to the Legal Enquiries (2000-2005), China Democracy and Law Press, 2006, pp.89.

② In the implementation of the constitution led by the administration, even by the people's government of the township, has the duty and obligation for constitutional compliance control. According to the *Circular of the State Council Concerning Printing and Circulation of Chinese Women's Development Plan and Chinese Children's Development Plan* (Guo Fa (2011) No.24), if the people's government of the township finds that the villagers' self-governance constitution and village regulations filed with it contravene the Constitution, laws, regulations and national policies, and contain the contents which discriminate against women or harm the legitimate rights and interests of women, it shall make appropriate corrections in a timely manner.

③ On November 19, 1983, in the *Circular Concerning the Stopping of land Sales and Leasing*, the State Council pointed out, "These acts severely violate the Constitution and must be resolutely stopped."

④ On July 17, 1992, in the *Circular of the State Council Concerning the Stopping of Examination and Approval of Nationality Towns*, the State Council stated that the establishment of nationality towns was not consistent with the Constitution of the People's Republic of China and must be resolutely stopped; otherwise, it would damage the sanctity of the Constitution of the People's Republic of China as the fundamental law of the state, and would cause chaos in the administrative division system and affect administrative management of the state.

(You Bu (1992) No.788), as a department under the State Council, the Ministry of Postal Service and Telecommunications pointed out, "If the people's courts require post and telecommunications departments to stop providing communication service for the reason of urging the party concerned to perform duties, such a requirement contravenes Article 40 of China's Constitution, post and telecommunications departments do not assist in enforcement", while the judicial organs did not raise objection against it, and the Supreme People's Court circulated this circular and required the courts at various levels to observe this circular.

1.2.2 Active implementation of the constitution

Passive implementation of the constitution is not the only way for implementing the Constitution, and all state organs are obligated to implement the Constitution. In the case of making laws, the legislative body must study how to implement the Constitution through legislation, while the administrative organs also have to consider the Constitution when taking actions; in particular, the administrative organs have to take constitutional issues seriously during participation in legislation.[①] Therefore, the constitutional review must not restrict other state organs from fully implementing the Constitution in a more appropriate way; instead, other state organs must be allowed to further fully implement some constitutional norms within the scope of their respective functions and powers.[②] However, in general, the space for active implementation of the Constitution is subject to the conditions of constitutional compliance established for passive implementation. If active implementation of the Constitution goes beyond that boundary, passive implementation of the Constitution is initiated to correct it so as to preserve the constitutional order; for example, if legislation implementation oversteps the scope permitted by the Constitution or fails to meet the normative requirements

① Louis Fisher and Neal Devins, "Political Dynamics of Constitutional Law", West Pub. Co., 1992, pp.10-11.

② Lawrence Gene Sager, Fair Measure: "The Legal Status of Underenforced Constitutional Norms", 91 Harv. L. Rev. 1212 (1978), Ernest A. Young, Popular Constitutionalism and the Underenforcement Problem: The Case of the National Healthcare Law, 75 Law & Contemp. Probs. 157-186, (2012).

of the Constitution, this constitutes violation of the Constitution.

Unlike the mode of implementation of the constitution in Western countries, the space for China's passive implementation of the Constitution is limited, but that for active implementation is relatively vast. This is because with the impact of the constitutional concept of the Soviet Union, China's constitutional philosophy is different from that in Western countries; one characteristic of such differences is that China deems the Constitution a fundamental law for materializing the ordinary laws. This philosophy dates back to Stalin's discourse about constitutions: "A constitution is the fundamental law and is not merely the fundamental law. A constitution does not exclude the routine legislation work of the future legislative body, and requires such work. A constitution provides a legal basis for the future legislative work of that body."① With its impact, China's Constitution contains a large number of directive norms which need to be unfolded and materialized by the ordinary laws. For these directive norms, M. Ulric Killion explained that China's Constitution placed emphasis on protecting active freedom such as social rights rather than passive freedom, and these articles required state organs to actively perform more constitutional obligations. Therefore, implementation of the constitution was necessary.② The most typical way to actively implement the Constitution is that the legislative body makes laws on the basis of the Constitution. Besides the legislative body making laws according to the procedural or substantive norms of the Constitution, the administrative organs also make decisions by observing the procedure and authority enshrined in the Constitution and performing the obligations prescribed by the Constitution. The judicial organ applies the Constitution within the scope of functions and powers specified in the Constitution mainly by explaining constitutional compliance in judicial

① In this regard, Zhang Youyu further explained, "a constitution is the fundamental law of the state rather than a complete collection of laws, so it cannot contain everything. Its implementation is based on the corresponding laws." See Zhang Youyu, Further Studying the New Constitution, Implementing the New Constitution, *China Legal Science*, 1984 (1).

② M. Ulric Killion, "China's Amended Constitution: Quest for Liberty and Independent Judicial Review", 4 *Washington University Global Studies Law Review* 43 (2005).

judgment to indirectly implement the Constitution during judgment.①

During more than 30 years of the implementation of China's Constitution, active implementation of the Constitution was dominated by legislative implementation. In this regard, the mainstream political discourse is that "implementation of the constitution is promoted by (making) complete laws."② China's legislative body often states that "This law is hereby enacted in accordance with the Constitution" in the general provisions. Such a statement is not common in foreign legislation. As shown by the statistical data concerning legislation since the implementation of the constitution, most of the legislation materialized the provisions of the Constitution.③ Legislative implementation mainly includes further materialization and systematization of the systems enshrined in the Constitution, materialization of the organizational norms and just norms of the Constitution through legislation, and the establishment of various systems of guarantee of basic rights. Specific forms include: (1) implementing the Constitution through framework legislation, and materializing various organizational norms and procedural norms for the operation of state power as enshrined in the Constitution.④ From the perspective of comparative law, China's Constitution is nothing more than a principle-oriented organizational procedural structure rather than a check and balance structure.⑤ This

---

① Zhang Xiang, "Two Kinds of Constitutional Cases: Possible Impact of the Constitution on Judicature from the Perspective of the Explanation of Constitutional Compliance", *China Legal Science*, 2008 (3).

② Xi Jinping, "Speech during the Meeting of the People from All Walks of Life in the Capital on Celebrating the 30th Anniversary of the Promulgation and Implementation of the Current Constitution" (December 4, 2012); Zhang Dejiang, Speech in the Legislative Working Meeting of the Standing Committee of the National People's Congress (October 30, 2013).

③ Legislative Planning Office of the Commission of Legislative Affairs of the National People's Congress, Legislation Statistics of the People's Republic of China, China Democracy and Law Press, 2008, Chapter Seven.

④ For example, the *Law on Regional National Autonomy* provides that the Law of the People's Republic of China on Regional National Autonomy is the basic law for implementing the system of regional national autonomy prescribed by the Constitution.

⑤ Jianfu Chen, "Chinese law: context and transformation", Leiden: Martinus Nijhoff Publishers, 2008, p.78.

characteristic determines that the organizational and procedural norms of the Constitution need to come into being through legislation. This framework legislation is different from the general legislation based on the legislative authority specified in the Constitution, and it is even considered as a legal norm with the nature of quasi constitution.[①] (2) Legalizing the abstract basic rights into legal rights of different types, and separately establishing different legal systems in the public law system and the private law system — on the one hand, legislation is conducted to establish the pubic law system for guaranteeing rights and restricting powers, such as the *Administrative Permission Law, Administrative Compulsion Law and Administrative Penalties Law*; on the other hand, legislation is carried out to confirm the private law system, and define the relations of rights and obligations among equal subjects. (3) The active guarantee system for basic rights is improved through legislation. Specifically, specific legislation is conducted to confirm the legal systems necessary for guaranteeing the basic rights, such as the judicial and litigation system, the social security system, the educational system. (4) The legal boundary for guaranteeing the basic rights is established. The basic rights prescribed by the Constitution merely represent a principle declaration and it is necessary to carry out legislation to legally define the scope of exercising various basic rights. However, as there is no constitutional compliance review of laws, no constitutional judgment standard is available for determining the legitimacy of such a legal restriction.

① Stephen M. Griffin, "American Constitutionalism: From Theory to Politics", Princeton University Press, 1996, p.54.

2. Practical Development of the Supervision System for the Implementation of China's Constitution

According to the Constitution, all state organs are obligated to implement the Constitution and must conduct activities within the scope of the Constitution. However, what if relevant state organs do not implement the Constitution, or even violate the Constitution? It is essential to strengthen supervision over the implementation of the Constitution. Therefore, an important measure specified in the *Decision of the Central Committee of the Communist Party of China on Some Major Issues Concerning Comprehensively Promoting Law-based Governance of the Country* adopted in the Fourth Plenary Session of the 18th Central Committee of the Communist Party of China was to intensify the implementation of the Constitution and improving the constitutional interpretation and supervision system. This measure serves as an important legal system for guaranteeing comprehensive implementation of the Constitution.

The formal legal document which earlier brought forward the establishment and improvement of the constitutional review system is the *Work Report of the Standing Committee of the National People's Congress* in 1998. This report explicitly stated, "supervision of the implementation of the constitution includes constitutional review of normative documents, including administrative regulations and local regulations, and is an important power of the National People's Congress.

This National People's Congress has enabled the filed local regulations to be preliminarily reviewed by special committees, and some special committees have put forward correctional opinions regarding the local regulations that are inconsistent with the Constitution and laws. However, there is a gap between this work and the requirements of the Constitution. It is necessary to further establish and improve the constitutional review system, and clearly specify the contents, form and procedure of constitutional supervision."① This is one of the few official statements about constitutional supervision, constitutional review and constitutional compliance review in China's existing formal legal documents.

On December 3, 2014, in the official written instructions on the Constitution Day, Xin Jinping stressed, "The Constitution is the fundamental law of the state, and the constitution for administering state affairs well and ensuring national security. It is the concentrated reflection of the Party and the people's will. It has the highest legal status, legal authority and legal validity." As shown, the word "legal" is used three times to emphasize the legal nature of the Constitution. During comprehensive implementation of China's Constitution, more emphasis is placed on legal implementation of the Constitution, especially the supervisory system for the implementation of the constitution. Therefore, taking the Constitution as the fundamental law will become the mainstream concept.

In October, 2014, the Fourth Plenary Session of the 18th Central Committee of the Communist Party of China vowed to improve the supervisory mechanism and procedure for the implementation of the constitution, and the mechanism for the interpretation of the constitution, which will become a key point of future legal construction in China.

In March, 2015, the *Work Report of the Standing Committee of the National People's Congress* stated, "It is necessary to improve the supervisory mechanism of the constitution of the National People's Congress and its Standing Committee, the procedural mechanism for the interpretation of the constitution, and establish the system of pledging allegiance to the Constitution. It is essential to earnestly carry out the filing review of normative documents, revoke and correct

① *Work Report of the Standing Committee of the National People's Congress* (1998).

unconstitutional normative documents according to the laws."

2.1 Institutional Design in the Text of China's Constitution

Article 27 of the Constitution adopted in 1954 reads: "The National People's Congress exercises the following functions and powers: (1) amending the Constitution; (2) enacting laws; (3) supervising the implementation of the Constitution..." Furthermore, this Constitution did not provide that the Standing Committee of the National People's Congress had the function and power of "supervising the implementation of the Constitution". In the community of constitutional jurisprudence, it is generally believed that this Constitution was a good constitution, but it was not really implemented. One important cause for failing to implement it was that the supervisory mechanism prescribed by this Constitution was not effectively implemented. Some scholars believed that the main cause for not effectively implementing this Constitution was that the text of this Constitution had no effective provision governing the mechanism for guaranteeing and supervising the implementation of the constitution; for example, there was no special body or procedure for supervising the implementation of the constitution. However, this was not the real cause because Article 27 of this Constitution explicitly provided that the National People's Congress supervised the implementation of this Constitution, while the National People's Congress failed to perform this duty for various reasons.①

As a socialist constitution, the Constitution adopted in 1954 affirmed China's fundamental political system — the system of a people's congress — and established the state organs, with the people's congresses at various levels as the core, based on the administrative, adjudication and procuratorial organs of the state at various levels, and provided for the basic rights and basic obligations of the citizens of the People's Republic of China; furthermore, it also had the corresponding institutional provisions for guaranteeing its own role of normalization

① Han Dayuan, "The Historical Status and Time Spirit of the Constitution Adopted in 1954", *China Legal Science*, 2014 (4).

and legal effect. Its main characteristics[1] are as follows:

First, the third paragraph of Article 27 of the Constitution adopted in 1954 reads: "The National People's Congress has the power to supervise the implementation of the Constitution." This provision was of great significance since it affirmed the requirement for implementing this Constitution, and granted the National People's Congress the power to supervise its implementation. Although it did not mention constitutional review, as shown by the behavioral characteristic that the National People's Congress should supervise the implementation of this Constitution, the following actions cannot be excluded while exercising the power to supervise the implementation of this Constitution: If noncompliance with this Constitution is found, it has the power to conduct a constitutional review of unconstitutional legal provisions or acts according to this Constitution, and draw relevant conclusions, or maintain the legal provisions or acts subject to supervision, or declare the legal provisions or acts subject to supervision as unconstitutional or invalid. Therefore, as a system, constitutional review was not denied in the Constitution adopted in 1954 and was indirectly included in the supervisory system for the implementation of the constitution.

Second, the fifth paragraph of Article 31 of the Constitution adopted in 1954 reads: "The Standing Committee of the National People's Congress has the power to supervise the work of the State Council, Supreme People's Court and the Supreme People's Procuratorate." This provision did not explicitly state that the Standing Committee of the National People's Congress should supervise the work of the State Council, Supreme People's Court and the Supreme People's Procuratorate in accordance with this Constitution; however, this Constitution was the legal basis for the Standing Committee of the National People's Congress to supervise the work of the State Council, Supreme People's Court and the Supreme People's Procuratorate. Such an interpretation is also rational and cannot be excluded. As indicated by Article 30, which reads: "The Standing Committee of the National People's Congress is the standing

① Mo Jihong, "The Historical Evolution, Problems and Developmental Trends of China's Constitutional Review System", *Theory and Practice of Constitutional Review* chiefly edited by Mo Jihong, Law Press China, 2006, Chapter Ten.

body of the National People's Congress", and the third paragraph of Article 27, which reads: "The National People's Congress has the power to supervise the implementation of the Constitution", the fifth paragraph of Article 31 of this Constitution actually granted the Standing Committee of the National People's Congress with the power to supervise the work of the State Council, Supreme People's Court and the Supreme People's Procuratorate in accordance with this Constitution. Therefore, it also implied that the Standing Committee of the National People's Congress conducted constitutional review of the work of the State Council, Supreme People's Court and the Supreme People's Procuratorate.

Third, the sixth paragraph of Article 31 of the Constitution adopted in 1954 reads: "The Standing Committee of the National People's Congress has the power to annul the decisions and orders of the State Council that contravene the Constitution, laws and decrees." In fact, this provision affirmed the power of the Standing Committee of the National People's Congress to conduct constitutional review of decisions and orders because the Standing Committee of the National People's Congress decided to annul the decisions and orders of the State Council that actually contravene the Constitution on the premise of the judgment that decisions and orders were unconstitutional. Therefore, if the Constitution adopted in 1954 is deemed to establish the content of the constitutional review system, it is clear that the Standing Committee of the National People's Congress has the power to conduct constitutional review of the decisions and orders of the State Council.

Fourth, the first paragraph of Article 49 of the Constitution adopted in 1954 reads: "The State Council adopts administrative measures, issues decisions and orders in accordance with the Constitution, laws and decrees, and reviews the implementation of these decisions and orders." This provision can be construed to contain the contents of constitutional review. First, according to this provision, the State Council must apply this Constitution to making administrative measures and issue decisions and orders, so the State Council certainly makes the judgment about compliance or noncompliance with this Constitution when making administrative measures and issuing decisions and orders. Second, the State Council has the power to review the implementation of decisions and orders. According to this provision, the State Council is bound to directly or indirectly review the implementation of relevant constitution articles when reviewing the implementation of decisions and orders.

Fifth, Article 100 of the Constitution adopted in 1954 reads: "Citizens of the People's Republic of China must abide by the Constitution and laws, observe labor discipline and public order and respect social ethics." The above provision explicitly showed observance of this Constitution as a legal obligation. This provision also laid a very good institutional foundation for guaranteeing the implementation of the constitution and establishing the constitutional review system.

Overall, the provision of the Constitution, concerning the constitutional review system, adopted in 1954 did not directly determine that a certain state organ had constitutional review power — the power of the Standing Committee of the National People's Congress to annul the decisions and orders that contravene the Constitution can be construed as a kind of constitutional review power—, and it mainly emphasized the necessity for strengthening and supervising the implementation of the constitution to guarantee the authority of this Constitution, and held that it was immature to take constitutional review as a constitutional system, or was merely an embryonic form of constitutional review. This was also very clear in the *Report on the Draft Constitution of the People's Republic of China* delivered by comrade Liu Shaoqi. With performance of duties prescribed by this Constitution, comrade Liu Shaoqi stressed in this report, "the Constitution must be observed by all of the people and all state organs. Deputies to the National People's Congress and local people's congresses at various levels and the working personnel of all state organs are the servants of the people, and all state organs are the organs serving the people therefore they are specially obligated to observe the Constitution and guarantee its implementation." Liu Shaoqi also vowed to fight against violations of this Constitution. He said, "Violations of this Constitution cannot be automatically eliminated after promulgation of the Constitution, but the Constitution provides us with a powerful weapon, enabling us to effectively get rid of these violations."[1]

The provisions of the Constitution, concerning constitution

---

[1] Mo Jihong, "Constitution Guide for Government and Citizens", Chinese People's Public Security University Press, 1999, pp.359-360.

implementation and supervision over constitution implementation, adopted in 1954 were affected and restricted by the historical conditions at that time. First, with the several years of its construction, new China restored and developed in its political, economic and cultural undertakings, for which the social order tended to become stable, and the political power was consolidated; in such a circumstance, it was necessary to recognize the achievements of the people's revolution in the form of a constitution, and take it as the legal basis for guiding new China to continue advancing. Therefore, in the process of drafting the first constitution, comrade Mao Zedong made very vivid descriptions of the significance of the first constitution and the necessity for observing it. In the 30th meeting of the Commission of the Central People's Government on June 14, 1954, Mao Zedong pointed out, "This draft constitution is completely feasible and must be implemented. Of course, now it is just a draft; once it has been adopted in the National People's Congress several months from now, it will become a formal constitution. Now we shall make preparations for its implementation. After its adoption, all the people across the country must implement it, especially the working personnel of state organs who must take the lead in implementing it which means everyone of you presents here today will implement it first. Failure to implement it amounts to violation of it."① Although comrade Mao Zedong used very plain language to equate "failure to implement the constitution" with "violation of the constitution", it was at least shown that the Party and state leaders attached great importance to the roles of the first constitution of new China in the process of drafting it. However, before long, the expansion of the anti-rightist movement caused setbacks in the guiding thought; as a result, although the constitutional articles and provisions existed, in practice, the guiding thought of the main leaders had a question about whether to act according to the constitution. For example, in the coordinated region head meeting held in Beidaihe in August, 1958, Mao Zedong said, "I participated in establishing the constitution, I cannot remember it. Comrade Liu Shaoqi once questioned: Was it rule of law or rule of man? In my opinion, it actually relied on

① Xu Chongde, "Constitutional History of the People's Republic of China", Fujian People's Publishing House, 2003, p.420.

man, while laws only served as a reference for man's actions."①

The current constitution adopted in 1982 is based on the Constitution adopted in 1954 and its all-round revision. On September 10, 1980, the 3rd Session of the 5th National People's Congress accepted the suggestion of the Central Committee of the Communist Party of China to pass the resolution concerning revision of the constitution and establishment of a Constitution Revision Committee. Ye Jianying, Chairman of the Standing Committee of the National People's Congress, served as Chairman of the Constitution Revision Committee, while Vice-chairmen Song Qingying and Peng Zhen served as Vice-chairmen of the Committee. The first meeting of the Constitution Revision Committee on September 15 decided to set up the Secretariat of the Constitution Revision Committee as the working body of the Committee responsible for this revision of the constitution. Hu Qiaomu served as Secretary General of the Constitution Revision Committee. Besides the basic work on constitutional revision, Hu Qiaomu mainly focused his attention on taking charge of drafting the *Decision on Some Historical Issues Concerning the Party since the Founding of New China*, so his schedule was very tight and his work was toilsome. After the *Decision on Some Historical Issues Concerning the Party since the Founding of New China* was passed in the Sixth Plenary Session of the 11th National Congress of the Communist Party of China, Hu Qiaomu fell sick and needed to recover, so he advised Deng Xiaoping to postpone the review of the constitution. Deng Xiaoping believed that it was essential to lose no time in revising the constitution and the review cannot be postponed, thus he talked with Peng Zhen and entrusted him to take charge of drafting the revision of the constitution.②

Afterwards, Peng Zhen was directly responsible for revising the constitution. Peng Zhen's line of thinking and plans were different from those of Hu Qiaomu to some extent. According to textual research, from June 27 to June 29, 1981, Peng Zhen attended the Sixth Plenary

---

① General Office of the Standing Committee of the National People's Congress, 40-year Development of the System of the People's Congress, China Democracy and Law Press, 1991, p.102.

② The Writing & Compilation Group for the Biography of Peng Zhen, Those days When Peng Zhen Took Charge of Drafting the 1982 Constitution, *The People's Congress of China*, 2012 (24).

Session of the 11th National Congress of the Communist Party of China, in which the *Decision on Some Historical Issues Concerning the Party since the Founding of New China* was passed; during this session, Hu Yaobang asked Peng Zhen: "Can the draft revision of the constitution be finalized by September? If not, it will be difficult to arrange the next year's work." Peng Zhen passed on Hu Yaobang's opinion to Wang Hanbin et al. on the morning of June 29; meanwhile, he proposed to revise the constitution on the basis of the Constitution adopted in 1954 and to develop a second plan.①

Starting from July, 1981, Peng Zhen began to take charge of an all-round revision of the constitution. Peng Zhen pointed out that the drafting of Constitution should be based on the the drafting of Constitntion in 1954. Deng Xiaoping agreed with this opinion and said, "Nearly 30 years have passed since 1954, the new constitution should take on a completely new look." There are three main reasons for the draft being based on the Constitution adopted in 1954: First, the basic principles prescribed by the Constitution adopted in 1954 were relatively appropriate; second, unnecessary debates can be avoided once the revision has been based on the Constitution adopted in 1954; third, it was conducive to finishing the task as soon as possible.②

---

① Ibid.

② Peng Zhen said, "Once constitution revision is based on the Constitution adopted in 1954, many troubles, submerged reefs and unnecessary debates can be avoided; for example, such issues as whether unicameralism or bicameralism is adopted, regional national autonomy, speaking out freely, airing views fully, holding great debates and writing big-character posters, the freedom to strike, whether or not to add a preamble, whether or not to establish the procuratorial organ, a 4-year term for deputies to the National People's Congress and provincial people's congresses, etc, were considered in the 1954 Constitution; if they are revised, the reasons should be specified; if their revision does not matter, they should not be revised. Why can consensus not be reached, do opinions vary and can the draft not be submitted after more than ten months of efforts by the Secretariat of the Constitution Revision Committee? This is because the issue concerning whether revision should be based on the 1954 Constitution has not yet been fully addressed. If it is determined to be based on the 1954 Constitution, the thinking will become clear and work can be carried out more quickly." The Writing & Compilation Group for the Biography of Peng Zhen, Those days When Peng Zhen Took Charge of Drafting the 1982 Constitution, *The People's Congress of China*, 2012 (24).

The Constitutional supervision system was an important hot topic during constitution drafting. When taking charge of the Secretariat of the Constitution Revision Committee, comrade Hu Qiaomu delivered a report on *Several Issues Concerning Constitutional Revision* to the Secretariat of the Central Committee, comrades Zhao Ziyang and Peng Zhen. Afterwards, he wrote the *Report on Some Issues Concerning Constitutional Revision*, including the conception and suggestions about improvement to the supervisory mechanism for the implementation of the constitution. As recorded by Wang Hanbin, "whether or not to set up a special body to guarantee the implementation of the constitution was the hottest topic for discussion from the beginning of constitution revision to the finalization of the draft revision...more opinions favored the establishment of a constitutional committee...the centralized plan was submitted, some leaders disagreed with it and believed that it was difficult to set up such a body, so it was shelved." "Many delegations also proposed establishing a constitutional committee, while the Working Group for Constitutional Revision conducted a study and comrade Hu Sheng gave an explanation in the presidium meeting." Thus deputies understood it and believed that it should be reflected by adding a new provision: "All acts which violate the Constitution and laws must be investigated and dealt with." Wang Hanbin had a comment: "This provision is very popular, but it is very difficult to implement it."①

According to a study conducted by Liu Songshan, failure to establish a constitutional committee was mainly attributable to the views and attitudes of important political figures of the special historical period.② Peng Zhen's opinions represented the mainstream opinions of relevant leaders at that time. Peng Zhen said, "Everyone is concerned with the implementation of the constitution and whether or not to set up an authoritative body to supervise its implementation. There is a constitutional committee in foreign countries, and grand justice is

① Wang Hanbin, "Interviews with Wang Hanbin — Experiencing Socialist Democracy and the Building of a Legal System in the New Period", China Democracy and Law Press, 2012.

② Liu Songshan, "1981: Shaped but Aborted Design of the Constitutional Committee", *Tribune of Political Science and Law*, 2010 (5).

established in some foreign countries like the USA and Pakistan. Do we adopt such a mode? This issue has been repeatedly considered during the drafting of the constitution. As we know, the 1954 Constitution was put aside during the Cultural Revolution. In fact, can this problem be solved, regardless of the organization? I think the answer is: not necessarily. I'm afraid that no organization has a higher power and prestige than the National People's Congress to manage this matter. According to the articles of the constitution, the National People's Congress and its Standing Committee have six special committees; in case the National People's Congress and its Standing Committee believe that there are constitutional violations, special committees will conduct relevant investigations. If there are constitutional violations, members of the Standing Committee of the National People's Congress, deputies, every citizen and every unit can report these violations, while the Standing Committee enables them to be investigated by special committees. Organizationally, this is relatively ideal. In addition, the people's congresses at various levels also have this duty. Of course, with the development of the situation, we can review whether to lay down a specific provision in the future."[①]

According to the records of constitutional revision, Hu Sheng shared the same views with Peng Zhen: "The supervisory tasks of the bodies similar to the constitutional committee in France and Italy are limited, while the implementation of the constitution in China is supervised by the National People's Congress and its Standing Committee, which actually play the roles of the constitutional court and the constitutional committee in some foreign countries. However, it is impossible for every article of the constitution, every state affair, and even the freedom and rights of every citizen to be guaranteed by a special body."[②]

① The Writing & Compilation Group for the Biography of Peng Zhen, Those days When Peng Zhen Took Charge of Drafting the 1982 Constitution, *The People's Congress of China*, 2012 (24).

② Liu Songshan, "Peng Zhen and Constitutional Supervision", *Journal of East China University of Political Science and Law*, 2011 (5).

2.2 Constitutional Basis for China's Constitutional Supervisory System

The current constitution was established after the guiding principle for the building of a socialist legal system — there must be laws to go by, the laws must be observed and strictly enforced, and lawbreakers must be prosecuted — was determined in the Third Plenary Session of the 11th Central Committee of the Communist Party of China, so it best sums up the experiences and lessons in building a socialist legal system in more than 30 years after the founding of new China, and provides relatively systematic and comprehensive norms for strengthening the measures for implementing the constitution and guaranteeing its implementation, laying the necessary legal foundation for developing the constitutional review system with Chinese characteristics.

Specifically, the 1982 Constitution specifies the following several principles and systems concerning the establishment of the constitutional review system with Chinese characteristics:①

First, it stipulates that the Constitution is a law and has the validity of the fundamental law as well as providing the constitutional basis for making legal judgments according to the Constitution.

The last paragraph of the preamble to the Constitution makes it clear that the Constitution is law, and stipulates that the Constitution has the supreme legal authority, so this provides the most basic legal basis for carrying out constitutional review, and the Constitution develops from the pure political program to the legal basis for judging whether people's acts are right or wrong, and the Constitution has the applicability of a law and the legal validity during its implementation. This paragraph reads: "The Constitution, in its legal form, affirms the achievements of the struggles of the Chinese people of all nationalities and defines the basic system and basic tasks of the State; it is the fundamental law of the State and has supreme legal authority. The people of all nationalities, all State organs, the armed forces, all political parties and public organizations and

① Mo Jihong, "The Historical Evolution, Problems and Developmental Trends of China's Constitutional Review System", *Theory and Practice of Constitutional Review* chiefly edited by Mo Jihong, Law Press China, 2006, Chapter Ten.

all enterprises and institutions in the country must take the Constitution as the basic standard of conduct, and they have the duty to uphold the sanctity of the Constitution and ensure its implementation."

The above provisions of the current constitution are of great significance. The 1952 Constitution, 1975 Constitution and the 1978 Constitution did not make it clear that the constitution was a law; therefore, although reinforcement of the implementation of the constitution was emphasized, its implementation was affected by the political situation because the constitution was too political to make effective legal judgment. With summarization of the past experience and lessons, the current constitution explicitly states that the Constitution is a law, showing a scientific and advanced understanding of the nature of the constitution, providing the constitutional basis for establishing the constitutional review system based on constitutional judgment.

Second, it stresses the principle of rule of law characterized by constitutional supremacy and the unification of the legal system, providing the necessary legal basis for conducting constitutional review of laws and regulations according to the Constitution.

Article 5 of the Constitution very explicitly defines the authoritative legal status of the Constitution as the fundamental law and the role of the Constitution in guaranteeing the unification of the legal system. These provisions present a basic legal standard for constitutional review. These provisions mainly cover the following five aspects:

(1) The People's Republic of China is ruled by law and is a socialist country under the rule of law;

(2) The state upholds the uniformity and dignity of the socialist legal system.;

(3) No laws or administrative or local rules and regulations may contravene the Constitution;

(4) All State organs, the armed forces, all political parties and public organizations and all enterprises and public institutions must abide by the Constitution and laws. All acts in violation of the Constitution and laws must be investigated and dealt with;

(5) No organization or individual is privileged to go above the Constitution and laws.

The above provisions specify the line of thinking that any violation of the Constitution must be investigated and dealt with, in other words, any unconstitutional law, regulation or act must be investigated and dealt with, and violation of the Constitution is an important concept and important judgment standard for guaranteeing the implementation of the constitution. Legally, the above provisions actually affirm the necessity for a constitutional review system.

Third, it establishes the institutional possibility of constitutional review in supervision over the implementation of the constitution.

In addition to emphasizing the principle that violation of the Constitution must be investigated and dealt with, the current constitution sets forth the specific system to ensure review and correction of constitutional violations. This is realized mainly by prescribing the power of the National People's Congress and its Standing Committee to supervise the implementation of the constitution; for example, Article 62 and Article 67 of the Constitution provide that the National People's Congress and its Standing Committee have the power to supervise the implementation of the constitution. Article 67 reads: "The Standing Committee of the National People's Congress supervises the work of the State Council, the Central Military Committee, the Supreme People's Court and the Supreme People's Procuratorate."

Fourth, it prescribes the requirements of constitutional compliance for state acts to prevent constitutional violations.

The current constitution stipulates explicit requirements of constitutional compliance for State acts. The first paragraph of Article 89 of the Constitution reads: "The State Council adopts administrative measures, enacts administrative rules and regulations and issues decisions and orders in accordance with the Constitution and laws." In fact, this provision specifies the requirement of constitutional compliance for the State Council to adopt administrative measures, enacts administrative rules and regulations and issues decisions and orders; in other words, such adoption, enactment and issuance must be based on the Constitution; otherwise, they will become null and void. Article 100 of the Constitution reads: "The people's congresses of provinces and municipalities directly under the Central Government and their standing committees may adopt local regulations subject to not contravening the Constitution and laws and administrative rules and regulations, and they must report such local regulations to the Standing Committee of the National People's Congress for the record."This provision explicitly stipulates the requirement of constitutional compliance that local regulations must not contravene the Constitution.

Fifth, it establishes the constitutional review mechanism.

When it comes to the legal mechanism for constitutional review, the current constitution does not stipulate the specific procedure for constitutional review, but it specifies several relevant systems so that they should be legally construed to include the function of constitutional review according to its intrinsic institutional functions; for example, Article 67 of the Constitution provides that the Standing Committee of the National People's Congress has the power to interpret the Constitution, and the procedure and result of constitutional interpretation show that it is inevitable for them to make a judgment about whether or not the interpreted matters violate the Constitution, so the constitutional interpretation mechanism is an important method of constitutional review. In addition, the current constitution also establishes the filing system as an institutional measure for constitutional review. According to Article 100 of the Constitution, the local regulations adopted by the people's congresses of provinces and municipalities directly under the Central Government and their standing committees shall be filed with the Standing Committee of the National People's Congress. According to Article 115 of the Constitution, the organs in national autonomous areas exercise the power of autonomy within the limits of their authority as prescribed by the Constitution, the *Law of the People's Republic of China on Regional National Autonomy* and other laws. With respect to whether or not the regulations on the exercise of autonomy and other separate regulations made in national autonomous areas — as the important form of exercising autonomy — comply with the Constitution, according to Article 116 of the Constitution, the regulations on exercising autonomy and other separate regulations of autonomous prefectures and counties must be submitted to the standing committee of the people's congresses of provinces or autonomous regions for approval before they come into effect, and they must be reported to the Standing Committee of the National People's Congress for the record. Obviously, the above filing system has the connotation that the filed regulations are to be reviewed for constitutional compliance.

Sixth, it affirms the legal effect that all laws which contravene the Constitution must be annulled.

According to Article 67 of the Constitution, the Standing Committee of the National People's Congress has the power to annul the administrative rules and regulations, decisions and orders of the State Council that contravene the Constitution and laws, and to annul the local regulations and decisions of the organs of the State power of provinces, autonomous regions, and municipalities directly under the Central Government that contravene the Constitution, laws or administrative rules and regulations. Obviously, the above provision affirms the power of the Standing Committee of the National People's Congress to conduct constitutional review of administrative rules and regulations, decisions, orders, local rules, regulations and decisions, and its power to annual the unconstitutional administrative rules and regulations, decisions, orders, local rules, regulations and decisions.

Seventh, it prescribes the obligations for guaranteeing the implementation of the constitution.

In order to guarantee the implementation of the constitution and prevent unconstitutional acts, the current constitution stipulates the obligations of different subjects for guaranteeing the implementation of the constitution, mainly including:

(1) General obligations of all organizations and individuals. The preamble to the Constitution reads: "The people of all nationalities, all State organs, the armed forces, all political parties and public organizations and all enterprises and public institutions in the country must take the Constitution as the basic standard of conduct, and they have the duty to uphold the sanctity of the Constitution and ensure its implementation."

(2) Obligations of deputies to the people's congresses. Article 67 of the Constitution reads: "Deputies to the National People's Congress must play an exemplary role in abiding by the Constitution and laws, keeping State secrets, and assisting in the implementation of the Constitution and laws in production, work and social activities."

(3) Obligations of local people's congresses. Article 99 of the Constitution reads: "Local people's congresses at various levels

must ensure the observance and implementation of the Constitution and laws and administrative rules and regulations in their respective administrative areas."

(4) Obligations of national autonomous areas. Article 115 of the Constitution reads: "The organs of self-government of the autonomous regions, autonomous prefectures and autonomous counties must exercise the functions and powers of local organs of State as specified in Section 5 of Chapter III of the Constitution. At the same time, they must exercise the power of autonomy within the limits of their authority as prescribed by the Constitution, the *Law of the People's Republic of China on Regional National Autonomy* and other laws and implement the laws and policies of the State in light of the existing local situation."

(5) Obligations of citizens. Article 53 of the Constitution reads: "Citizens of the People's Republic of China must abide by the Constitution and laws."

The above provisions governing observance of the obligations prescribed by the Constitution stress the constitutional thinking that "no violation of constitution is permitted".

Overall, the current constitution has relatively comprehensive and systematic stipulations of the constitutional review system; as shown by the above provisions of the current constitution, China's constitutional review system has basically taken shape at the institutional level. Specifically, there are the following several characteristics:

(1) The current constitution further enriches the contents of the concept of constitutional violation, and many provisions of the current constitution establish the concept that "contravening the Constitution is not permitted"; for example, Article 5 of the Constitution reads: "No laws or administrative or local rules and regulations may contravene the Constitution." Furthermore, according to Article 100 of the Constitution, local regulations must not contravene the Constitution. Contravening the Constitution is an important principle and method for judging constitutional violation.

(2) It delimits the boundary of the concept of constitutional violation, and strictly restricts constitutional violations to constitutional articles to prevent the generalization of the concept of constitutional violation; for example, the fifth paragraph of Article 5 of the Constitution reads: "No

organization or individual is privileged to go above the Constitution and laws." Obviously, this paragraph takes the text of the Constitution as the basis for exercising rights, and going beyond the text of the Constitution leads to denying its legitimacy — constitutional violation.

(3) Constitutional violations must be investigated and dealt with. Based on recognizing the concept of constitutional violation, the current constitution explicitly denies and requires disciplinary action against unconstitutional acts; for example, the fourth paragraph of Article 5 of the Constitution reads: "All acts in violation of the Constitution and laws must be investigated and dealt with." This paragraph reflects the basic legal attitude, in the current constitution, that the legitimacy of unconstitutional acts is denied.

(4) Constitutional violations are solved by the National People's Congress and its Standing Committee. In order to address the concept of constitutional violation in an institutionalized, procedure-based way, the current constitution provides that the National People's Congress and its Standing Committee have the power to supervise the implementation of the constitution; in particular, the Standing Committee of the National People's Congress has the power to interpret the Constitution. This means that the Standing Committee of the National People's Congress interprets and makes the relevant decision to determine whether there is constitutional violation during the implementation of the constitution. As indicated by the above provision of the Constitution, the current constitution does not passively leave constitutional violations uncurbed; instead, it provides the organizational guarantee for constitutional review by requiring the establishment of a constitutional body of interpretation.

(5) The current constitution further makes it clear that all unconstitutional laws, regulations and acts are null and void and must be annulled, and it denies various incorrect concepts which hold that the Constitution is merely a political program and ignore the authority of the Constitution in practice by insisting that observance of the Constitution does not matter; for example, according to the eighth paragraph of Article 67 of the Constitution, the Standing Committee of the National People's Congress has the power to annul the local regulations and decisions of the organs of State power of the provinces, autonomous regions, and municipalities directly under the Central Government that

contravene the Constitution. Obviously, under the current constitution, the unconstitutional local regulations and decisions are annulled as the legal consequence, while those who commit unconstitutional acts may be removed from office as the legal consequence of their acts; for example, according to Article 63 of the Constitution, the National People's Congress has the power to remove from office the President and the Vice-president of the People's Republic of China, the Premier, Vice-premiers, State Councillors, Ministers in charge of ministries or commissions, the Auditor-General and the Secretary-General of the State Council, the Chairman of the Central Military Commission and other members of the Commission, the President of the Supreme People's Court and the Procurator-General of the Supreme People's Procuratorate. Clearly, the constitutional review prescribed by the current constitution has been fully institutionalized, and it not only affirms the concept of constitutional violation, but also defines the ways for dealing with violations of the constitution and the legal consequences resulting from those violations. This was not fully embodied in the 1954 Constitution.

Therefore, it is fair to say that the constitutional review system was not really established in China until the 1982 Constitution. It should also be noted that the Standing Committee of the National People's Congress never conducted a formal legally valid constitutional review according to the Constitution in more than 30 years since the adoption of the 1982 Constitution. As shown by this fact, although constitutional review was institutionalized in the 1982 Constitution, the procedure and level of the said institutionalization are not very high; in particular, there are many defects in the constitutional review procedure and specific operational mechanism so that the mechanism fails to function effectively.

2.3 Development of the Constitutional Supervisory System Led by the National People's Congress

After the promulgation of the Constitution, the National People's Congress attached great importance to supervision over the implementation of the constitution. However, some provisions and measures may be inconsistent with the Constitution, which was a problem that had to be opportunely solved at that time. Therefore, in February, 1983, Vice-chairman Peng Zhen pointed out that politics and law departments should actively and systematically check whether or not there is noncompliance with the new constitution in work, and it was necessary to lose no time in earnestly correcting all noncompliance with the new constitution. The Standing Committee of the National People's Congress believes that all State organs, armed forces, political parties, social groups and all grass-roots units must act in strict compliance with the Constitution without any exception. Local people's congresses and their standing committees must ensure that the Constitution is observed and enforced within their administrative areas. Deputies to the people's congresses at various levels should play an exemplary role in observing and enforcing the Constitution. All acts in violation of the Constitution must be investigated and dealt with. This is an important aspect of earnestly guaranteeing the implementation of the constitution.[①]

Meanwhile, the Central Committee of the Communist Party of China attached great importance to supervision over the implementation of the constitution. With a view to ensuring strict implementation of the personnel appointment and removal procedure prescribed by the Constitution, the *Circular of the Central Committee of the Communist Party of China Concerning Strict Compliance with Legal Procedures in the Case of Appointing and Removing the Leaders of State Organs* (April 26, 1984) reads: "The leaders of State organs at various levels must be elected by the people's congresses at the corresponding levels or appointed and removed by their standing committees; this is the power granted to the people's congresses at various levels and their standing committees by the Constitution and laws. Our Party leads the people to make the Constitution and laws and also leads the people to enforce the Constitution and laws." The *Constitution of the Communist Party of China* revised and adopted in the 12th National Congress of the Communist Party of China reads: "The Party must conduct its activities within the framework of the Constitution and laws of the country." No activity of the Party organizations must run counter to the Constitution and laws; this is a basic principle which must be observed in the political

① Work Report of the Standing Committee of the National People's Congress (1983).

life of the Party and the State, to which the Party committees at various levels must pay extreme attention.

In the work report in 1985, the Standing Committee of the National People's Congress summarized the moves of local people's congresses at various levels in correcting unconstitutional acts and affirmed some moves. The work report pointed out, "Some provincial people's governments annulled, at their own discretion, the local regulations approved by the standing committees of provincial people's congresses. The standing committees of some county people's congresses made local regulations. Some counties posted notices to recruit the directors of bureaus of county governments. Some localities appointed township heads. Without election by the people's congresses or decisions made by the standing committees of the people's congresses, some localities announced appointment of the leaders of State organs which must be elected by the people's congresses or appointed by the standing committees of the people's congresses. These acts did not comply with laws. All standing committees of local people's congresses concerned took measures to make corrections after discovering them. The cases in which various localities took measures to correct the acts inconsistent with laws were appropriately reported by the *Work Newsletter* of the General Office of the Standing Committee, playing an active role in guaranteeing law enforcement and enhancing the people's legal awareness."①

In April, 1985, Peng Zhen further summed up supervision over the implementation of the Constitution in various areas, and pointed out, "There are various kinds of constitutional violations, including those at severe, moderate and mild levels. If all constitutional violations are submitted to the Standing Committee of the National People's Congress, the Standing Committee will be overwhelmed. So who should handle different constitutional violations? On the one hand, it is necessary to make all of the people become familiar with, get used to, consciously execute, safeguard and supervise the Constitution. This is the greatest power. On the other hand, some constitutional violations can be dealt with at the county or provincial levels, and only major constitutional

① Work Report of the Standing Committee of the National People's Congress (1985).

violations are handled by the people's congress. The National People's Congress and its Standing Committee mainly focus on supervising the major unconstitutional incidents having a vital bearing on national security, national economy and the people's livelihood."①

In May, 1985, when holding a conversation with Vice-chairman of the Standing Committee of the National People's Congress, part of the people in charge of the Law Committee, the Financial & Economic Committee, the Commission of Legislative Affairs of the Standing Committee of the National People's Congress, and the Secretary-general of the Standing Committee of the National People's Congress, Peng Zhen stated, "Two years have passed since the adoption of the Constitution, and it is time to deal with constitutional violations. If we do not deal with the constitutional violations which should be dealt with, we will feel guilty about not performing our duties to the fullest. It is unnecessary to deal with a large number of constitutional violations, and we should figure out facts through one or two typical cases and deal with it or them according to legal procedure, so as to educate everyone to abiding by the Constitution and laws; in this regard, we can't afford to be careless."②

One of the tasks for the Standing Committee of the National People's Congress in 1986 was supervision over the implementation of the constitution and correction of constitutional violations. In 1986, the Standing Committee of the National People's Congress supported and urged some localities to correct the acts inconsistent with the Constitution and laws; for example, in some localities, the cadres who should have been appointed and removed by the people's congresses according to laws were appointed and removed by the standing committees of the people's congresses. In some localities, the powers of the people's congresses were not respected, with the cadres elected by the people's congresses and appointed by the standing committees of the people's congresses being randomly replaced and frequently transferred. In some localities, the personnel of the standing committees of the people's congresses who exercised their power to vote down the

① Liu Songshan, "Peng Zhen and Constitutional Supervision", *Journal of East China University of Political Science and Law*, 2011 (5).

② The Writing & Compilation Group for the Biography of Peng Zhen, Chronological Biography of Peng Zhen, Central Party Literature Press, 2012, p.315.

requested appointment were criticized at will. The Standing Committee of the National People's Congress required relevant localities to make necessary treatments and act in strict compliance with laws.①

The Standing Committee of the Sixth National People's Congress once considered establishing a special supervisory body to supervise the implementation of the constitution. In its work report, the Standing Committee of the Seventh National People's Congress once vowed to set up a special body for supervision. According to the proposal made by comrade Peng Zhen, the chairman's meeting decided that Vice-chairmen Chen Pixian and Huang Hua would take charge of conducting surveys on the supervision exercised by the National People's Congress and put forward opinions about strengthening such supervision. In response to these opinions, arrangements were made in the *Work Report of the Standing Committee of the National People's Congress*: "It is necessary to proceed from reforming the political system and building the socialist democracy to further deepen the understanding of the supervision exercised by the National People's Congress. The supervision exercised by the National People's Congress and its Standing Committee is the national authoritative supervision conducted on behalf of the people's interests and will, and it is essential for the normal operation of the national mechanism. Correct supervision is conducive to improving the decision-making system, reducing errors and ensuring smooth socialist modernization, reform and opening up. With the separation of the functions of the Party from those of the government and reinforcement of governmental functions, the supervisory power of the National People's Congress and its Standing Committee becomes more important. It is necessary for the National People's Congress to carefully summarize the supervisory experience in several years, set up a special supervisory body, and develop the supervisory regulations to more clearly define the contents, scope, procedure and mode of supervision so that supervision is gradually institutionalized and standardized. Fundamentally addressing supervisory issues depends upon intensifying the reform of the political structure."② In the following two years, the National People's Congress

① Work Report of the Standing Committee of the National People's Congress (1986).

② Work Report of the Standing Committee of the National People's Congress (1988).

attached great importance to constitutional supervision.

The *Work Report of the Standing Committee of the National People's Congress (1989)* pointed out, "An important power of the Standing Committee of the National People's Congress is supervision over the implementation of the constitution. In the past year, the Standing Committee carried out some work on supporting and urging relevant localities and departments to correct the acts which violated the Constitution and laws, but the work should be further improved and intensified...in the future, the Standing Committee should further strengthen supervision over the implementation of the Constitution and laws: reviewing administrative regulations and local regulations; listening to the reports of the State Council and its relevant departments, the Supreme People's Court and the Supreme People's Procuratorate on law enforcement; selectively checking the enforcement of some major laws; urging relevant departments to earnestly correct violations of the Constitution and laws."①

Since 1990, the arrangements for constitutional supervision exercised by the National People's Congress have become more concrete and profound. According to the arrangements and plans of the Standing Committee, the Standing Committee of the National People's Congress should beef up supervision over the implementation of the Constitution and laws, and once violations of the Constitution and laws are found, it should urge relevant law enforcement departments to make timely corrections; in particular, it should intensify constitutional compliance control of the legal system. The *Work Report of the Standing Committee of the National People's Congress (1990)* pointed out, "As more and more administrative regulations and local regulations are made, they play important roles in national political life, economic and social life, but there is some nonconformity among some of them, even some of these regulations contravene laws of the state. In order to safeguard the unity of the legal system, relevant special committees should review the local regulations filed with the Standing Committee, and the administrative regulations made by the State Council; if regulations are found to contravene the Constitution and laws, they should put forward handling

① Work Report of the Standing Committee of the National People's Congress (1989).

opinions and report to the Standard Committee for making a decision. This work remains a vulnerable spot, so it is necessary to seriously improve and strengthen it."①

In 1991, the *Work Report of the Standing Committee of the National People's Congress* continued to focus on filing a review: "Supervising the implementation of the constitution is an important power of the Standing Committee of the National People's Congress. Safeguarding the sanctity of the Constitution and ensuring effective implementation of the Constitution has a vital bearing on the long-term interests of all of the people and is the fundamental guarantee for national political, economic and social stability. The Standing Committee should intensify supervision over the implementation of the constitution. All State organs, armed forces, political parties, social groups, enterprises and public institutions and citizens must abide by the Constitution. All acts which violate the Constitution must be investigated and dealt with. The Standing Committee should step up efforts to review the administrative regulations made by the State Council and the local regulations filed with the Standing Committee of the National People's Congress, and annul or order them to correct the regulations which contravene the Constitution and laws according to the laws and the procedure specified in the work focus rules of the Standing Committee of the Seventh National People's Congress. This work has not yet earnestly been carried out and it is necessary to take measures and develop systems to improve it according to the Constitution and laws in the future."②

The opinions and suggestions from all sectors of the society promoted the improvement of the constitutional supervisory mechanism. In order to build and improve the constitutional supervisory system, under the unified arrangements made by the Central Committee of the Communist Party of China, the Standing Committee of the Seventh National People's Congress started drafting the supervision law. One of the important political driving forces was the suggestion by the Central Committee of the Communist Party of China concerning the enactment of the supervision law. In the *Decision Concerning Reinforcing the*

① Work Report of the Standing Committee of the National People's Congress (1990).

② Work Report of the Standing Committee of the National People's Congress (1991).

Ties with the Masses adopted on March 12, 1990, the Sixth Plenary Session of the 13th Central Committee of the Communist Party of China pointed out, "It is necessary to establish and improve the inner-party supervisory and the non-party supervisory system. It is suggested that the Standing Committee of the National People's Congress should draw up the supervisory law for work supervision and legal supervision." In May, 1990, according to the requirements of the Central Committee of the Communist Party of China, the Standing Committee of the Seventh National People's Congress set up the supervisory law drafting group, and started the first round of drafting the supervisory law. Under the direct leadership of the Chairman, the Vice-chairmen and the Secretary-General of the Standing Committee of the National People's Congress, the supervisory law drafting group, consisting of Zhou Jie, Gu Angran, Liu Zheng and Cheng Xiangqing, was established. Cheng Xiangqing also served as the leader of the secretariat group and was responsible for specific drafting work. Besides the research backbone from the research office, including Wang Min, Guo Linmao, Wu Wentai, Zheng Yunhai, Liu Yiqian, the drafting group also included a number of scholars who were experts on the Constitution and legal research from the Commission of Legislative Affairs of the Standing Committee of the National People's Congress, the Chinese Academy of Social Sciences and local people's congresses such as Zhang Qingfu, Gu Xiuyi, Xu Anbiao, Zhou Xiaohong, Tan Quan, Xu Gongxun. Extensive survey and research and in-depth feasibility studies were conducted before drafting. Opinions were solicited from various parties after drafting. Besides solicitation of opinions from special committees of the National People's Congress, the Commission of Legislative Affairs of the Standing Committee of the National People's Congress, the General Office and bureaus (offices), Peng Chong, Vice-chairman of the Standing Committee of the National People's Congress, also specially chaired a symposium with participation by people in charge of the organs of the people's congresses in ten provinces and municipalities to carry out discussions and feasibility studies. Ye Lin, Vice-chairman of the Financial & Economic Committee of the National People's Congress, chaired a symposium with participants from the ministries and commissions under the State Council to solicit opinions. A North China financial and economic working symposium with participation of people in charge of the financial and economic committees of 12 provincial people's congresses was also held to conduct a heated debate on the exposure draft of the supervisory law, in which participants actively put forward revision opinions while recognizing the exposure draft. Meanwhile, the supervisory law drafting group solicited opinions from many scholars by means of visits, correspondence and symposiums. After repeated deliberations were made and the draft was changed numerous times, the *Law of the People's Republic of China on the Supervision of the National People's Congress and Its Standing Committee* (revised draft, October 27, 1990) was finalized.①

In September, 1996, under the direct leadership of the Chairman and the Executive Vice-chairmen of the Standing Committee of the National People's Congress, the leading group for drafting the law of supervision of the Standing Committee of the National People's Congress, for which Cao Zhi, Secretary-General of the Standing Committee of the National People's Congress, and Xue Ju, Chairman of the Law Committee of the National People's Congress, were responsible, was set up. The leading group had the supervisory law drafting office consisting of personnel from the Research Office of the General Office of the Standing Committee of the National People's Congress, the National Law & Administrative Law Office and the Economic Law Office of the Commission of Legislative Affairs of the Standing Committee of the National People's Congress, the Judicial Office of the Committee for Internal and Judicial Affairs of the National People's Congress, the Planned Budget Office of the Financial & Economic Committee of the National People's Congress, research offices of the Standing Committees of Shandong Province and Shannxi Province. Cheng Xiangqing concurrently served as Director of the drafting office, while Yin Zhongqing (Deputy Director of the Research Office) et al. served as deputy directors, and Yin Zhongqing, Li Qiusheng, Li Bojun, Guo Linmao, Fang Weilian, Xu Anbiao, Yao Sheng, Yu Jianwei, Ouyang Kegang and Zhao Ruilin were the main survey personnel and writers. With intense work for more than two years, the *Law of the People's*

① Cheng Xiangqing, "Three Things I Experienced in Constitutional Jurisprudence Research", *Chinese Yearbook of Constitutional Law (2006)*, Law Press China, 2006.

Republic of China on Supervision of the National People's Congress and Local People's Congresses at Various Levels (the seventh internal draft) was finalized on November 30, 1997.

The drafting of the above supervisory law was very complicated and tortuous. An important line of thought for this drafting was separate incorporation of "supervision over the implementation of the constitution" as one chapter. Specific chapters were structured as follows:[①]

Chapter One General Provisions, Subjects, Principles and the Scope of Supervision

Chapter Two Supervision over the implementation of the constitution, the procedure for review of normative documents including administrative regulations

Chapter Three Examination of law enforcement

Chapter Four Deliberating and hearing the work reports of the State Council, the Supreme People's Court and the Supreme People's Procuratorate

Chapter Five Reviewing the report on a planned budget and its execution

Chapter Six Deliberating the work reports of the State Council, the Supreme People's Court and the Supreme People's Procuratorate

Chapter Seven Deliberating the work reports of the working personnel elected and appointed by the People's Congress

Chapter Eight Accepting whistle-blowing, appeals and complaints, exercising supervision over individual cases

Chapter Nine Supervisory mode and means such as inquiry, investigation of specific problems, removal

According to the records made by Cheng Xiangqing, relevant departments spoke highly of the draft supervisory law: "A meeting of financial and economic committees of North China people's congresses was held in Tianjin, in which participants highly commended the draft. Comrade Peng Chong organized a meeting with the participation of

① Li Peng, "Legislation and Supervision — Li Peng's Diary of Work in the National People's Congress", Xinhua Publishing House, China Democracy and Law Press, 2006, p.530.

people in charge of the standing committees of the people's congresses of ten provinces and municipalities in North China and Northeast China to discuss and revise the articles of the draft. The draft was also approved by Wan Li, Chairman of the Standing Committee of the National People's Congress. Although it was not ultimately introduced, it offered much beneficial experience for subsequent drafting of the supervisory law and subsequent legislation regarding supervision."①

Some changes occurred in the drafting of the supervisory law during the term of the Standing Committee of the Ninth National People's Congress.

In July, 1999, according to the *Legislation Plan of the Standing Committee of the Ninth National People's Congress* and the opinions from various parties, the Standing Committee of the Ninth National People's Congress set up the supervisory law drafting group for the third time, initiating the third round of drafting. After efforts were made for more than three years, repeated surveys were conducted and the draft was changed 12 times, the *Law of the People's Republic of China on the Supervision of the National People's Congress and Local People's Congresses At Various Levels (Draft)* was finalized. The greatest difference between this draft and the one made during the term of the Standing Committee of the Eighth National People's Congress was that the draft did not incorporate constitutional supervision as a special chapter — of course, there was no committee on constitutional supervision.

How to deal with the relations between the Party's leadership and supervision of the National People's Congress was an important topic during the drafting of the above supervisory law. Li Peng, Chairman of the Standing Committee of the National People's Congress, once reported and communicated this issue to Jiang Zemin, General Secretary of the Communist Party of China, many times.② This issue was also repeatedly mentioned during discussions about the draft in the Standing Committee

---

① Cheng Xiangqing, "Reviews the Course of Enactment of China's First Supervisory Law: An Important Milestone", *Legal Daily*, September 15, 2014.

② See Li Peng, "Legislation and Supervision — Li Peng's Diary of Work in the National People's Congress", Xinhua Publishing House, China Democracy and Law Press, 2006, p.531, p.558.

of the National People's Congress. Li Peng once stressed many times on different occasions that the supervision of the National People's Congress must be under the Party's leadership. During discussion and deliberation on the draft supervisory law, Li Peng emphasized, "The National People's Congress is an organ of power relative to other State organs. The National People's Congress carries out work under the leadership of the Communist Party of China. Some people believed that the National People's Congress was the highest organ of State power, thus it was also the highest supervisory body. This is inconsistent with the reality; although the National People's Congress is the highest organ of State power, its work is under the leadership of the Communist Party of China. This is the characteristic of Chinese politics. Without this principle, the relationships between the Party and the National People's Congress could not be properly handled and duly put in place, and the work on various aspects could not be done well. If the work of the National People's Congress weakens rather than strengthens the Party's leadership, the National People's Congress runs counter to China's system. That's why I agree less with the view that only the National People's Congress enjoys the supremacy and has a higher reputation than the Party in the minds of the people. And I believe that the National People's Congress should not be the highest supervisory body. In China, the National People's Congress is an organ of State power under the Party's leadership, and the Party's leadership does not mean that the Party directly orders the National People's Congress, but means that the Party group of the National People's Congress exercises leadership over the work of the National People's Congress and converts the Party's propositions into the will of the State according to a legal procedure."①

Moreover, another institutional difficulty for the constitutional and legal supervision led by the National People's Congress is how to deal with the relationship between the National People's Congress and other State organs. During the drafting of the supervisory law, relevant leaders repeatedly stressed, "The National People's Congress "shares

① Li Peng, "Legislation and Supervision — Li Peng's Diary of Work in the National People's Congress", Xinhua Publishing House, China Democracy and Law Press, 2006, pp.562-563.

the same stage" with the State Council, the Supreme People's Court and the Supreme People's Procuratorate", "the National People's Congress must not exceed its powers, but must play the role of supervision", "the National People's Congress shall exercise supervision with suitable methods in an appropriate way", "the National People's Congress is not opposite to the State Council, the Supreme People's Court and the Supreme People's Procuratorate, and they share the work and cooperate with one another under the leadership of the Communist Party of China for the common goal."① In this regard, when speaking in the Ninth Meeting of the Standing Committee of the National People's Congress on April 29, 1999, Li Peng expounded this issue in a relatively systematic way. He pointed out, "In order to strengthen the supervision of the National People's Congress, the understanding of the supervision of the National People's Congress must first of all be intensified. Exercise of the power of supervision by the National People's Congress is the important contents of law-based governance of the country by the people led by the Party and the important embodiment of the people being the masters of the country. Meanwhile, it must be noted that the supervision over the State Council, the Supreme People's Court and the Supreme People's Procuratorate by the National People's Congress is essentially different from the restraints upon the government as exercised by the parliament in Western countries. China's State organs are established and operated under the principle of democratic centralism and work closely in cooperation with a due division of labor under the Party's leadership rather than under the tripartite political system. The supervision of the National People's Congress aims at urging the administrative, adjudication and procuratorial organs of the State to carry out law-based administration, keep judicial justice and improve the work. In this sense, supervision also supports the work of these State organs."②

① Li Peng, "Legislation and Supervision — Li Peng's Diary of Work in the National People's Congress", Xinhua Publishing House, China Democracy and Law Press, 2006, pp.531-560.

② ditto, pp.537-538.

2.4 Current Operation of China's Constitutional Supervision System

The 1982 Constitution establishes the system of constitutional supervision, but the degree of institutionalization of constitutional supervision is not very high, mainly characterized by the following aspects: The submission and hearing procedure for constitutional supervision is unclear; the institutional links among various systems for constitutional supervision are insufficient; various systems for constitutional supervision are scattered and mutually independent during the implementation of the constitution, and these systems cannot be connected through a unified effective legal procedure. Therefore, it is very difficult to initiate the procedure for constitutional supervision. In order to overcome this drawback, the *Legislation Law of the People's Republic of China* (the "Legislation Law") enacted in 2000 shows great progress in the procedure-based development of the system of constitutional supervision.

Article 90 of the Legislation Law in 2000[①] reads: "When the State Council, the Central Military Committee, the Supreme People's Court, the Supreme People's Procuratorate, and the Standing Committees of the People's Congresses of provinces, autonomous regions and municipalities directly under the Central Government believe that administrative regulations, local regulations, the regulations on the exercise of autonomy and separate regulations contravene the Constitution and laws, they may make a written request to the Standing Committee of the National People's Congress for review, and the working body of the Standing Committee must hand over this request to the relevant special

---

① Article 98 of the Legislation Law revised and adopted by the National People's Congress in March, 2015 reads: "When the State Council, the Central Military Committee, the Supreme People's Court, the Supreme People's Procuratorate, and the Standing Committees of the People's Congresses of provinces, autonomous regions and municipalities directly under the Central Government believe that administrative regulations, local regulations, the regulations on the exercise of autonomy and separate regulations contravene the Constitution and laws, they may make a written request to the Standing Committee of the National People's Congress for review, and the working body of the Standing Committee must hand over this request to the relevant special committees for review and comments."

committees for review and comments." "When other State organs, social groups, enterprises, public institutions or citizens not enumerated above believe that administrative regulations, local regulations, the regulations on exercising autonomy and separate regulations contravene the Constitution and laws, they may make a written proposal to the Standing Committee of the National People's Congress for review, and the working body of the Standing Committee must study this proposal, and where necessary, it must hand the proposal over to the relevant special committees for review and comments."

At least the above provisions of the Legislation Law explicitly stipulate the following several procedures and systems, and further improve the system of constitutional supervision.[①]

First, the Legislation Law establishes the procedure for initiating constitutional supervision and increases the possibility that the constitutional body is able to exercise constitutional supervision. Before the Legislation Law was promulgated, the procedure for initiating constitutional supervision was unclear — the 1982 Constitution does not explicitly stipulate such a procedure, nor do other relevant laws and regulations. The initiation procedure of constitutional supervision which may legally exist and can be institutionally affirmed may merely be attached to the process in which the National People's Congress and its Standing Committee supervise the implementation of the constitution; in other words, constitutional supervision fully depends upon the National People's Congress and its Standing Committee. Legally, once the National People's Congress and its Standing Committee find constitutional violations during the supervision over the implementation of the constitution, they will be bound to review these constitutional violations according to their functions and powers, and draw a review conclusion or provide a relevant constitutional interpretation about whether or not the Constitution has been violated. Such an initiation procedure of constitutional supervision very easily leads to passivism of an initiation procedure of constitutional supervision. In other words, if

---

① Mo Jihong, "The Historical Evolution, Problems and Developmental Trends of China's Constitutional Review System", *Theory and Practice of Constitutional Review* chiefly edited by Mo Jihong, Law Press China, 2006, Chapter Ten.

the National People's Congress and its Standing Committee are unwilling to or do not initiate the procedure of constitutional supervision, it would be very difficult to implement the legally valid constitutional supervisory activity in practice though the Constitution stipulates the system of constitutional supervision. Article 90 of the Legislation Law thoroughly changes the situation where there is no initiation procedure for constitutional supervision. According to this provision, the activity of constitution supervision can be initiated in at least two ways — first, the State Council, the Central Military Committee, the Supreme People's Court, the Supreme People's Procuratorate, and the Standing Committees of the People's Congresses of provinces, autonomous regions and municipalities directly under the Central Government may make a written request regarding constitutional supervision to the Standing Committee of the National People's Congress for initiating the procedure of constitutional supervision; second, other State organs, social groups, enterprises, public institutions and citizens may make a written request regarding constitutional supervision to the Standing Committee of the National People's Congress for initiating the procedure of constitutional supervision. Both initiation procedures can ensure that the relevant working body of the Standing Committee of the National People's Congress with the power of constitutional supervision must take certain measures to deal with the relevant request or suggestion concerning constitutional supervision. Such a procedure of initiation makes up for the drawback that the National People's Congress and its Standing Committee are merely relied upon to initiate the procedure when exercising their power to supervise the implementation of the constitution, lowers the threshold for constitutional supervision and increases the opportunities for the Standing Committee of the National People's Congress to exercise the power of constitutional supervision.

Second, the Legislation Law further defines the scope of the objects of constitutional supervision and restricts the objects of constitutional supervision to administrative regulations, local regulations, the regulations on the exercise of autonomy and separate regulations, so it avoids the situation where the objects of constitutional supervision are so uncertain and their scope is so wide as to lose the institutional capability for constitutional supervision in practice. The objects of constitutional supervision requested through two initiation procedures of constitutional supervision prescribed by the Legislation Law only include administrative regulations, local regulations, the regulations on the exercise of autonomy and separate regulations, while other legal forms are not subject to constitutional supervision as requested through the initiation procedures prescribed by the Legislation Law.

Third, those entitled to request constitutional supervision must separately make a request for constitutional supervision according to the Legislation Law rather than initiating constitutional supervision at will, and must raise a written request or suggestion for constitutional supervision.

Fourth, the constitutional supervisory activity is conducted by a special body; according to the Legislation Law, with respect to the written request or suggestion for constitutional supervision, review should be carried out by special committees of the National People's Congress.

Fifth, constitutional supervision must be accompanied by a relevant conclusion. One of the most important characteristics of the provisions of constitutional supervision of the Legislation Law is that a specific opinion is required for the request and suggestion regarding constitutional supervision — the request and suggestion for constitutional supervision raised according to the Legislation Law is not merely an expression in the general sense of political supervision; instead, such a request and suggestion must be carefully studied to put forward specific solutions. After the constitutional supervision procedure is initiated, the body with the power of constitutional supervision must take certain measures to give an official reply and conclusion in response to the request and suggestion regarding constitutional supervision.

Article 90 of the *Legislation Law of the People's Republic of China* shows a big stride forward in improving the constitutional supervision system prescribed by China's Constitution so as to develop the concept of constitutional violation from the legal level to the practical level, and it actively promotes the initiation of the constitutional supervision procedure — the most influential case concerns three doctors of law who submitted a proposal to the Standing Committee of the National People's Congress for initiating a constitutional review of the system of receiving and sending back urban vagrants and beggars in the case of Sun Zhigang, a university graduate working in Guangzhou, who was beaten to death by the working personnel responsible for receiving and sending back urban vagrants and beggars in 2003.[①]

On May 14, 2003, three doctors of law, Yu Jiang, Teng Biao and Xu Zhiyong, faxed, in the name of a Chinese citizen, a *Proposal Concerning Review of the Measures for Receiving and Sending Back Urban Vagrants and Beggars* to the Commission of Legislative Affairs of the Standing Committee of the National People's Congress, suggesting that the Standing Committee of the National People's Congress should exercise constitutional supervision over the system of receiving and sending back these people. The three doctors of law pointed out: "According to Article 37 of the *Constitution of the People's Republic of China*, the personal freedom of citizens of the People's Republic of China is inviolable. No citizen may be arrested except with the approval of or by decision of a people's procuratorate or by decision of a people's court, and arrest must be made by a public security organ. Unlawful detention and deprivation or restriction of a citizen's personal freedom by other means is prohibited, and unlawful search of a citizen's body is prohibited. According to Article 9 of the *Administrative Penalties Law of the People's Republic of China*, the administrative penalties for restricting personal freedom are only prescribed by laws. According to Article 8 and Article 9 of the *Legislation Law of the People's Republic of China*, the compulsory measures and penalties for depriving a citizen of their political rights and restricting their personal freedom are only based on laws. Therefore, the provisions concerning restriction of a citizen's personal freedom in the *Measures for Receiving and Sending Back Urban Vagrants and Beggars* issued by the State Council in 1982 and the detailed rules for their implementation contravene the Constitution, the Administrative Penalties Law and the Legislation Law, so we suggest that a constitutional and law violation review of the *Measures for Receiving and Sending Back Urban Vagrants and Beggars* should be conducted." Those three doctors of

① Mo Jihong, "The Historical Evolution, Problems and Developmental Trends of China's Constitutional Review System", *Theory and Practice of Constitutional Review* chiefly edited by Mo Jihong, Law Press China, 2006, Chapter Ten.

law were not the first citizens who requested constitutional supervision over the objects of constitutional supervision prescribed by Article 90 of the Legislation Law according to the Legislation Law after enactment of the Legislation Law; however, their submission of this proposal exerted a huge impact on society so that the general public realized that, in the institutional sense, the initiation procedure of constitutional supervision specified in the Legislation Law can bring about the best practical activity for requesting constitutional supervision. Although the relevant department of the Standing Committee of the National People's Congress did not make an explicit reply to those three doctors of law, a direct consequence was that Chinese Premier Wen Jiabao signed No.381 Decree of the State Council to announce the implementation of the *Administrative Measures for Assistance of Urban Vagrants and Beggars without Assured Living Sources* ("these Measures") on June 20, 2003. These Measures came into force as of August 1, 2003. According to them, the *Measures for Receiving and Sending Back Urban Vagrants and Beggars* issued by the State Council in May, 1982 were repealed simultaneously. From the perspective of "golden mean" and "good intention toward others" as stressed in Chinese traditional legal culture, in fact, the case where the State Council took the initiative to repeal the *Measures for Receiving and Sending Back Urban Vagrants and Beggars* which contravened the Constitution meant that those three doctors of law had reached the goal of requesting constitutional supervision. Therefore, in practice, the initiation procedure of constitutional supervision specified in Article 90 of the Legislation Law can supervise the unconstitutional regulations to some extent, and undoubtedly, the Legislation Law can play a very important role in promoting constitutional supervision from institutional regulation to legal practice.

After the Legislation Law established two legal procedures for initiating constitutional supervision, in order to further improve the procedure of constitutional supervision so that it becomes a repeatable and convenient constitutional system, the 40th Chairman's Meeting of the Standing Committee of the 10th National People's Congress completed the revision of the *Working Procedure for Filing a Review of Administrative Regulations, Local Regulations, the Regulations on the Exercise of Autonomy, Separate Regulations and Special Economic*

Zone Regulations (*the "Working Procedure for Filing Review of Regulations"*) and adopted the *Working Procedure for Filing Review of Judicial Interpretations* on the morning of December 16, 2005 so as to further develop and improve the system for filing a review of regulations and judicial interpretations and safeguard the unity of the national legal system. Given that the Standing Committee of the National People's Congress has set up a regulation filing review body in the Commission of Legislative Affairs, the revised *Working Procedure for Filing a Review of Regulations* provides that where the State Council, the Central Military Committee, the Supreme People's Court, the Supreme People's Procuratorate, and the Standing Committees of the People's Congresses of provinces, autonomous regions and municipalities directly under the Central Government believe that regulations contravene the Constitution or laws, they may make a written review request to the Standing Committee of the National People's Congress, and after the relevant department of the General Office of the Standing Committee receives and registers it, it should report it to the Secretary-General for approval before forwarding it to the relevant special committee for review in conjunction with the Commission of Legislative Affairs. Where other State organs, social groups, enterprises, public institutions and citizens not enumerated above believe that regulations contravene the Constitution or laws, and offer a written suggestion for review to the Standing Committee of the National People's Congress, the Commission of Legislative Affairs must receive, register and study it; where necessary, it should report it to the Secretary-General for approval before forwarding it to the relevant special committee for review. The revised *Working Procedure for Filing a Review of Regulations* also provides that where a special committee believes that the filed regulations contravene the Constitution or laws, it may take the initiative to review them, and put forward a written opinion regarding the review in conjunction with the Commission of Legislative Affairs; where the Commission of Legislative Affairs believes that the filed regulations contravene the Constitution or laws, it should take the initiative to review them, and may put forward a written suggestion and report it to the Secretary-General for approval before forwarding it to the relevant special committee for review. With regard to correction of the regulations which contravene the

Constitution or laws, the revised *Working Procedure for Filing a Review of Regulations* stipulates three steps: First, communicating and holding a consultation with the legislative organ; second, putting forward a written opinion regarding the review through the relevant special committee, requiring the legislative organ to make a correction; third, where the legislative organ does not make a correction after the above work, the regulations which contravene the Constitution or laws should be annulled with deliberation and decision of the Standing Committee.

In order to safeguard the unity of the national legal system, the 40th Chairman's Meeting of the Standing Committee of the 10th National People's Congress also adopted the *Working Procedure for Filing a Review of Judicial Interpretations.* The *Working Procedure for Filing a Review of Judicial Interpretations* provides that the judicial interpretations made by the Supreme People's Court and the Supreme People's Procuratorate should be filed with the Standing Committee of the National People's Congress within 30 days from the day of promulgation. Where State organs, including the State Council, social groups, enterprises, public institutions and citizens, believe that judicial interpretations contravene the Constitution or laws, they may make a request or suggestion for review to the Standing Committee of the National People's Congress. In addition, the *Working Procedure for Filing a Review of Judicial Interpretations* also specifies specific provisions for submission, reception and review of judicial interpretations, passive review and active review, the procedure for correcting the judicial interpretations which contravene the Constitution or laws.

3. Measures and Suggestions for All-round Implementation of China's Constitution

Both the life and the authority of the Constitution lie in implementation.

Comprehensive implementation of the Constitution is the primary task and basic work for promoting law-based governance of the country in an all-round way and accelerating the building of a law-ruled China. Implementation of the Constitution means that the Constitution is applicable to the real life and effectively plays its real role. Implementation of the constitution in a broad sense means that the contents of the Constitution is implemented in real life, while implementation of the constitution in a narrow sense means that State organs materialize the contents of the Constitution within the scope of their respective functions and powers according to the procedure specified by laws.

3.1 Basic Experience in Current Constitution Implementation in China

First, the Party's leadership should be upheld. The preamble to China's Constitution reads: "The people of all nationalities, all State organs, the armed forces, all political parties and public organizations and all enterprises and institutions in the country must take the Constitution as the basic standard of conduct, and they have the duty to uphold the sanctity of the Constitution and ensure its implementation." The establishment, revision and implementation of the Constitution embody the Party's leadership. In this regard, Peng Zhen pointed out: "Implementation of the constitution mainly relies upon State organs, especially the organizations of the Communist Party of China." The Party plays the core role of leader in grasping the overall situation and coordinating the various parties to support the organs of power, administrative organs, adjudication and procuratorial organs of the State to carry out their work in an independent, responsible and coordinated way in accordance with the Constitution and the laws. This is a political implementation mode, while the Party's leadership serves as a political guarantee for the implementation of the constitution.

Second, the implementation of the constitution is guaranteed through legislation. As the fundamental law, the Constitution plays the leading role in the legal system, which is a legal implementation mode. The implementation of the constitution based on legislation is a basic experience since the promulgation and implementation of the current constitution. The legislative bodies at various levels have made a numerous laws and regulations according to their legislation authority granted by the Constitution, while the basic spirit and principles prescribed by the Constitution are implemented in a relatively sufficient way through specific legislation. The legislative bodies work on promoting the implementation of the constitution through a complete set of laws to shape a socialist legal system with Chinese characteristics.

3.2 Two Key Issues Concerning the Implementation of China's Constitution

First, China's Constitution explicitly stipulates the mechanism for supervision for the implementation of the constitution and grants the National People's Congress and its Standing Committee the duty and power to supervise its implementation; however, in reality, some constitutional violations still exist and the supervisory mechanism for the implementation of the constitution has not yet been fully initiated and effectively operated. In response to such a situation, the Central

Committee has put forward, many times, the reform goal for improving the supervisory mechanism for the implementation of the constitution. In the constitution revision symposium in 1999, Jiang Zemin pointed out: "We should further foster the authority of the Constitution in the whole society, establish and improve a powerful supervisory mechanism for the implementation of the constitution." In the symposium, in celebrating the 20th anniversary of the promulgation and implementation of the Constitution, Hu Jintao pointed out: "It is necessary to lose no time in studying and improving the mechanism for constitutional supervision, and further clarify the procedure for constitutional supervision so that all unconstitutional acts can be opportunely corrected. The National People's Congress and its Standing Committee should proceed from the fundamental interests of the country and the people to fully guarantee the citizens' freedom and rights prescribed by the Constitution during legislation; it is essential to earnestly supervise the implementation of the constitution, resolutely redress the unconstitutional acts, and faithfully perform the function of interpreting the Constitution to make necessary interpretations and explanations about the issues in the implementation of the constitution so that the Constitution can be better implemented." In the symposium, in celebrating the 30th anniversary of the promulgation and implementation of the Constitution, General Secretary Xi Jinping stressed: "The National People's Congress and its Standing Committee as well as relevant supervisory bodies of the state should perform the duty for constitutional and legal supervision, strengthen supervision and inspection of the constitution and law enforcement, improve the supervisory mechanism and procedure, uncompromisingly correct the unconstitutional and unlawful acts." The Third Plenary of the 18th Central Committee of the Communist Party of China emphasized: "It is necessary to further improve the mechanism and procedure for supervising the implementation of the constitution, and elevate all-round implementation of the Constitution to a new level." Therefore, improvement of the mechanism of supervision of the implementation of the constitution is a key issue for the implementation of the constitution.

Second, an accurate understanding of the meaning of relevant constitutional provisions in legal practice is another key issue for the implementation of China's Constitution. The Constitution is the fundamental law of the state and should be implemented by special laws. The implementation of the Constitution covers the whole process of law enforcement. Law enforcement is based on a correct understanding of the Constitution and laws. As explicitly prescribed by Article 67 of China's Constitution, the Standing Committee of the National People's Congress exercises the power to interpret the Constitution. Laws are made according to the Constitution. Many legal issues are addressed by accurately understanding the meaning of the articles of the constitution; for example, Article 9 of the Constitution explicitly provides that all mineral resources, water, forests, mountains, grassland, unreclaimed land, beaches and other natural resources are owned by the State. However, in order to understand the scope of natural resources in legal practice, there is an urgent need for the organ of power to authoritatively interpret and define Article 9 of the Constitution.

3.3 Ten Suggestions for All-round Implementation of China's Constitution

As was pointed out at the Third Plenary Session of the 18th Central Committee of the Communist Party of China: "We should further improve the supervisory mechanism and procedure of the implementation of the constitution, and upgrade all-round implementation of the Constitution to a new level. We should establish and improve a system which society adheres to, observes, maintains and applies the Constitution and laws. Everyone is equal before the law. No organization or individual has the privilege of going above the Constitution and laws. All unconstitutional and unlawful acts must be investigated and dealt with." A comprehensive implementation of the Constitution should be promoted regarding the following ten aspects:

First, the Central Committee of the Communist Party of China should. exercises more leadership and further carries out an overall coordination of the implementation of the constitution. According to China's Constitution, all State organs and social organizations are obligated to guarantee the implementation of the constitution. The Party's leadership is the fundamental guarantee for the implementation of the constitution. The Party organizations at various levels should play the core role of leader in grasping the overall situation and coordinating various parties, providing the organizational guarantee for the implementation of the constitution. A special coordinating body for the implementation of the constitution may be established within the Party to exercise overall leadership and push forward the implementation of the constitution in a coordinated way.

Second, the implementation of the constitution should be promoted by further improving the legislation. Although China's socialist legal system has taken shape, some drawbacks still exist in this legal system in terms of the supervision mechanism for constitution implemetation, for example, there are inconsistencies among some legal provisions; some laws at lower levels conflict with the laws at higher levels. In order to comprehensively strengthen and improve the legislation, it is necessary to observe the systems and principles established by the Constitution, and build a mechanism that provides for optimization in order to continuously improve the socialist legal system, boosting all-round implementation of the Constitution to a new level.

Third, a mechanism for the concurrent promotion of legal interpretation and judicial interpretation should be established. According to China's existing system of legal interpretation, the Standing Committee of the National People's Congress once made an authoritative legal interpretation about the *Criminal Law*, the *Basic Law of the Special Administration Regions* and other laws. In legal practice, many legal issues are also constitutional issues, and some legal issues should be addressed by correctly understanding the meaning of the Constitution first; for example, the constitutional provision that public property is inviolable should be understood in the case of making a law regarding real rights. Therefore, where it is necessary to interpret legal provisions, relevant constitutional provisions should be interpreted so that the law enforcement organs can correctly understand the meaning of the law and the implementation of the Constitution in law enforcement would be promoted.

Fourth, the contents of the implementation of the constitution should be added into the annual work report of the Standing Committee of the National People's Congress. According to the Constitution, the

Standing Committee of the National People's Congress has the power to supervise the implementation of the constitution. The implementation of the Constitution should become the next focus in the work of the Standing Committee of the National People's Congress. Therefore, the Standing Committee of the National People's Congress should regularly summarize the implementation of the constitution and supervision over the implementation of the constitution, and report it to the National People's Congress.

Fifth, the mechanism for the review of the constitutional and legal compliance of laws and regulations should be improved. China's Constitution stipulates the mechanism for the review of the constitutional compliance of laws and regulations; however, as an operable procedural provision is unavailable, such a review mechanism is only at the stage of internal operations and a decision regarding its handling has not yet been publicly made. China's legal system has taken shape, but some legal norms within the legal system still conflict with the laws at higher levels, thus it is necessary to further optimize the legal system through the review mechanism. It is suggested that experience should be summarized to improve the relevant procedure and comprehensively initiate the mechanism for the review of laws and regulations.

Sixth, the *Basic Law of the Special Administrative Regions* should be interpreted based on the Constitution so as to reflect the constitutional spirit and uphold the authority of the Constitution. China's Constitution is operative in special administrative regions mainly by means of the basic law. Therefore, there is a misunderstanding in practice and it is believed that the Constitution is not legally valid in special administrative regions. In order to uphold the authority of the Constitution and dispel the misunderstanding of relevant aspects, constitutional provisions should be directly cited to interpret the basic law so as to reinforce the implementation of the Constitution in special administrative regions.

Seventh, a mechanism for the review of the constitutional and legal compliance of the rules and regulations of the Party should be established and improved. A review mechanism within the Party should be put in place to ensure that the regulations and normative documents of the Party made by the Commission for Discipline Inspection of the Central Committee of the Communist Party of China, central departments, the

Party committees of provinces, autonomous regions and municipalities directly under the Central Government comply with the Constitution and laws.

Eighth, the Party's leadership in and overall planning of legislation should be further strengthened. Policies are transcribed into the Constitution and laws so that major decisions and the latest positions of the Party are timely, effectively expressed through the Constitution and laws of the state and become the constitutional and legal basis for leading and regulating various kinds of work. This is an important institutional measure for guaranteeing the political leadership of the Party and ensuring that the Party conducts activities within the scope of the Constitution and laws.

Ninth, the Constitution should be revised and improved to create the favorable conditions for a comprehensive implementation of it. According to Article 5, Article 62 and Article 67 of China's Constitution, all State organs, the armed forces, political parties, social groups, enterprises and public institutions must abide by the Constitution and laws; the National People's Congress and its Standing Committee have the power to supervise the implementation of the constitution; the Standing Committee of the National People's Congress has the power to interpret the Constitution. However, with respect to the way to supervise the implementation of the constitution and interpret it, it is necessary to carry out a top-level design of the basic system and procedure for constitutional supervision and constitutional interpretation. Therefore, it is suggested that the Constitution should be revised and improved to further materialize and standardize the principal requirements for supervision over the implementation of the constitution and turn them into procedure, making them operable, thus creating the favorable conditions for the implementation of the constitution.

Tenth, theoretical research on the establishment of a special constitutional supervisory committee should be strengthened. In the annex to the *Supplementary Suggestions Concerning Revision of Part of the Constitution — the Explanatory Notes for Suggestions Concerning Revision of Part of the Constitution*, the Central Committee of the Communist Party of China pointed out, in March, 1993, that "According to Article 70 of the Constitution, the National People's

Congress may establish a special constitutional supervisory committee, and the Constitution may not incorporate a provision in this regard." The establishment of a special constitutional supervisory committee is beneficial to pushing forward the supervision over the implementation of the constitution from the perspective of the modernization of the national governance system and governance capacity, but there are some theoretical difficulties in establishing a constitutional supervisory committee, such as the relationship between the constitutional supervisory committee and the Party's leadership, the relationship between the constitutional supervisory committee and the system of the people's congress, the relationship between the constitutional supervisory committee and other special committees, what is subject to the supervision of the constitutional supervisory committee and how this committee exercises supervision, the composition, functions and powers of the constitutional supervisory committee; an in-depth theoretical research on these issues is required.

4. Measures and Suggestions for Improving China's Constitutional Supervision System

Improving the supervision system for the implementation of China's constitution, upholding the authority of the Constitution, defending the sanctity of the Constitution and guaranteeing the implementation of the constitution are the important means for governing the Party, the country and the army under the new situation, and also the inevitable requirement for governing the country according to the laws in an all-round way and promoting the modernization of national governance.

General Secretary Xi Jinping pointed out: "Guaranteeing the implementation of the constitution ensures the realization of the people's fundamental interests. As long as we earnestly respect and effectively implement the Constitution, there is an assurance that the people are the masters of the country, and the undertakings of the Party and the country can develop smoothly. On the contrary, if the Constitution is ignored, weakened, or even destroyed, the people's rights and freedom cannot be guaranteed, and the undertakings of the Party and the country will suffer setbacks."

4.1 The Necessity for Improving China's Constitutional Supervision System①

The promulgation and implementation of China's current constitution vigorously promote reform, opening-up and socialist modernization as well as the building of a socialist country under the rule of law. This strongly pushes forward the development of the cause of human rights, and vigorously safeguards national unity, ethnic solidarity and social stability, exerting a very profound impact on China's political, economic, cultural and social life. Meanwhile, we must be keenly aware that some problems and drawbacks still exist in comprehensively promoting the implementation of the constitution. At present, the following urgent problems need to be solved in implementing China's Constitution:

First, the appointment and removal of personnel violates the procedure prescribed by the Constitution. The Party committees in some localities directly appointed and removed the leading cadres by sidestepping the procedure prescribed by the Constitution; for example, the Party committees removed the officials elected by the people's congresses not in accordance with the statutory procedure. The system of the people's congress is China's fundamental political system. The third paragraph of Article 3 of the Constitution reads: "All administrative, judicial and procuratorial organs of the State are created by the people's congresses to which they are responsible and by which they are supervised." The Party committees in some localities removed, at their own discretion, the officials elected by the people's congresses by ignoring the Constitution and local organizational law as well as the removal power of the people's congresses in violation of the Constitution; this is wrong due to a lack of constitutional thinking. In some localities, standing committees were established at the people's congresses at the township level, or township heads were directly elected by circumventing the procedure at the people's congresses in violation of the Constitution and election law; these acts violated the Constitution and

① Xi Jinping, "Speech in the Meeting of the People from All Walks of Life in the Capital on Celebrating the 30th Anniversary of the Promulgation and Implementation of the Current Constitution" (December 4, 2012).

should be corrected.

Second, the basic rights of citizens are infringed upon. For example, the Constitution provides for freedom and privacy of correspondence, but some administrative and judicial organs restrict citizens' freedom and privacy of correspondence by bypassing the procedure prescribed by the Constitution, and some conduct excessive legislation to restrict these basic rights; for example, the fourth paragraph of Article 180 of the *Securities Law* stipulates that the China Securities Regulatory Commission has the power to access and copy the data, including the property rights registration and correspondence records relating to the events under investigation. However, Article 40 of the Constitution reads: "Freedom and privacy of correspondence of citizens of the People's Republic of China are protected by law. No organization or individual may, on any grounds, infringe upon the citizens' freedom and privacy of correspondence, except in cases where, to meet the needs of State security or of a criminal investigation, public security or procuratorial organs are permitted to censor correspondence in accordance with the procedures prescribed by the law." In addition, there are also similar legal provisions, in the *Prison Law*, which violate the Constitution.

Third, there are contradictions among laws. Conflicts and inconsistencies still exist within the legal system, and a unified review should be properly conducted according to the Constitution. China's current legal system consists of the legal norms involving different sectors and fields. These legal norms are still inconsistent with the Constitution to some extent, and there are conflicts and inconsistencies among some legal norms. These conflicts and inconsistencies within the legal system should be governed and integrated by the standard of the Constitution so as to shape a legal system with rigorous internal logic. In some localities, regulations were adopted to carry out regional protectionism, bringing obstacles to the formation of a uniform, open, competitive, orderly market order across the country and damaging the unity of the rule of law across the country.

Fourth, some high-ranking leading cadres violated the Constitution and destroyed the constitutional order; for example, when Bo Xilai served as the Party Secretary of Chongqing Municipality, he wielded his personal authority above and beyond the Constitution and laws, set up an "independent kingdom", abused State power, thus wreaking havoc on the constitutional order. As a high-ranking leading cadre in the political and legal work led by the Party, Zhou Yongkang turned a blind eye to the Constitution and laws, bent laws for personal gains, abused public power for personal purposes and trampled on the constitutional principles.

At present, in China, the supervisory mechanism and systems for guaranteeing the implementation of the constitution are deficient; constitutional and legal violations still exist in some departments and localities; some public servants, especially leading cadres, often commit unconstitutional and unlawful acts in China. We must attach great importance to these constitutional and legal violations and practically solve them through institutional improvement.

As explicitly stipulated by China's Constitution, the National People's Congress and its Standing Committee are responsible for supervising the implementation of the constitution. In the meeting celebrating the 30th anniversary of the promulgation and implementation of the current Constitution, General Secretary Xi Jinping pointed out: "The National People's Congress and its Standing Committee as well as relevant supervisory organs of the State should perform the duty of constitutional and legal supervision, strengthen the supervision and inspection of the constitution and law enforcement, improve the supervisory mechanism and procedure, and resolutely correct the unconstitutional and unlawful acts." The Third Plenary Session of the 18th Central Committee of the Communist Party of China vowed to further improve the mechanism and procedure of the supervision over the implementation of the constitution, to elevate comprehensive implementation of the Constitution to a new level. The Fourth Plenary Session of the 18th Central Committee of the Communist Party of China put "improvement of the system concerning the constitutional supervision of the National People's Republic of China and its Standing Committee" on the important agenda of all-round promotion of law-based governance of the country.

In our opinion, the key to upholding the authority of the Constitution, correcting the unconstitutional acts and boosting law-based governance of the country lies in improving the system of supervision of the implementation of China's constitution. It is necessary to build a system of supervision for the implementation of the constitution with Chinese characteristics based on careful research and scientific appraisal as soon as possible, and set up a special supervisory body for the implementation of the constitution within the National People's Congress that can supervise the implementation of the constitution, thus promoting and guaranteeing comprehensive implementation of the Constitution at the institutional and mechanism level.

4.2 The Great Significance of the Establishment and Improvement of the Supervision System for the Implementation of China's Constitution

The authority and life of the Constitution lie in its implementation. The implementation of the Constitution requires an effective guarantee of supervision. The system of supervision of the implementation of the constitution is an indispensable important part of the democratic political system with Chinese characteristics, and is the top-level design crucial for pushing forward law-based governance of the country in an all-round way. It is an institutional arrangement for urgently accelerating the constitution-based governance and the fundamental institutional guarantee for achieving prolonged stability of the country. Improving the system of supervision of the implementation of China's constitution is the important way to strengthen the Party's leadership and increase the level of law-based governance; it is the inevitable requirement for comprehensively promoting the law-based governance of the country and an important guarantee for boosting the modernization of the national governance.

First, improving the system of supervision of the implementation of China's constitution is conducive to reinforcing the leadership of the Communist Party of China, upholding the authority of the Party, consolidating the governing status of the Party, and enhancing the Party's capability for governance based on the Constitution and laws. During wartime, as the revolutionary political party, the Party mainly relied on guns to seize political power; during peacetime, as the governing party, the Party has mainly depended upon "knife handle" — the rule of law

— to govern the country and handle State affairs. The Constitution is the fundamental law and the general constitution for the Party to lead the people and manage State affairs. Upholding the authority of the Constitution amounts to preserving the authority of the common will of the Party and the people. Safeguarding the sanctity of the Constitution is equivalent to defending the dignity of the common will of the Party and of the people. Under the new situation, in order to better perform the major duty of governing and allowing the country to prosper, the Party must strengthen its self-discipline according to the Party's constitution and govern the country according to the Constitution. Law-based exercise of State power is the key to governing the country according to laws, and it is the basic principle and important means for the Party to govern the country and handle State affairs. In order to exercise State power according to the laws, it is necessary to first of all abide by the Constitution in that exercise; in order to promote law enforcement, it is essential to implement the Constitution first.

China's Constitution reflects, in the form of fundamental law, the achievements made by the people under the leadership of the Party during the revolution, construction and reform; it establishes the leading position, resulting from historical evolution and the people's choice, of the Communist Party of China. Improving the system of supervision of the implementation of China's constitution is of great significance for reinforcing the Party's leadership, consolidating the governing status of the Party and enhancing the Party's capability for exercising State power according to the Constitution.

(1) Upholding the leadership of the Communist Party of China is one basic principle affirmed by the preamble to China's Constitution. Improving the system of supervision of the implementation of China's Constitution is conducive to proceeding from compliance with the fundamental law of the state to adopt the operable system and procedure of supervision of the implementation of the constitution in order to ensure that the spirit of the whole Constitution, including its preamble, is respected, all constitutional principles are observed, and all constitutional provisions are implemented, so as to effectively consolidate the leading status of the Party, maintain the authority of the Party in governance, beef up the constitutional foundation for governance of the country

and exercise the State power under the system of one-party leadership by the Communist Party of China, and strongly refute the domestic and foreign hostile forces who vilify and attack the constitutional compliance of the Party-led governing system.

(2) China's Constitution is the highest legal form for transposing the Party's policies and guidelines for governing the country and handling State affairs into State will; it shows distinctive political value guidance and guarantees people's democracy. Improving the system of supervision of the implementation of China's constitution is beneficial to comprehensively activating the political value and the function of the implementation of the Constitution, and turning China's Constitution from a "soft idle one", mistaken by some people, into a feasible "rigid one", thus further strengthening and guaranteeing a high unity of the Party's leadership and the Constitution, converting major policies and guidelines of the Party into the highest will of the State through the Constitution. The mechanism of supervision of the implementation of the constitution ensures that State organs at various levels earnestly implement the Constitution and all public servants exemplarily abide by the constitutional norms.

(3) China's Constitution serves as the fundamental standard for activities of all State organs, the armed forces, political parties, social groups, enterprises and public institutions. Improving the system of supervision of the implementation of China's constitution helps reinforce a unified supervision over major decisions made and political acts committed by the above bodies according to the Constitution, and conduct a unified review of major decisions and legislative decisions made by local governments; it is conducive to making a unified arrangement for supervision over the operation of national judicial power, and upholding the authority of the Central Committee, ensuring a smooth implementation of the decisions made by the Central Committee, and guaranteeing the Party's absolute leadership in the army, political and legal forces, and preventing some administrative departments and local governments from acting only for their respective purposes rather than in a coordinated way.

(4) China's Constitution is the fundamental law of the State, while all laws, administrative regulations and local regulations should not

contravene the Constitution. China's Constitution is also the general constitution for administering State affairs and ensuring national security; all regulations and documents of the Party should be consistent with the Constitution and should not run counter to the constitutional principles and spirit. Improving the supervision system for the implementation of China's constitution, and establishing a mechanism for a coordinated constitutional review of the Party's regulations, documents and national laws helps combine the Party's leadership with constitution-based governance of the country at the level of institutional norm, guarantee coordination and intrinsic unity between the Party's regulation system and the national legal system, and ensure that the Party's regulations and documents comply with the Constitution and laws, thus enhancing the scientificity and effectiveness of the Party's law-based exercise of State power.

Second, improving the supervision system for the implementation of China's constitution is favorable to preserving and improving the socialist system with Chinese characteristics, and propelling the modernization of the national governance system and governance capacity. Laws are the vital means for governing the country, while the rule of law is an important support for the national governance system and governance capacity. The Constitution is the important mark of national governance modernization since it has the highest legal status, legal authority, legal validity, it has a vital bearing on the overall situation and exerts a fundamental, long-term impact, and has a profound implication for stability. In order to carry forward the modernization of national governance, shape a well-developed, scientific, standardized and effective national governance system to ensure that the systems for national governance are more sophisticated and well-functioning, most fundamentally, it is necessary to uphold the authority of the Constitution, guarantee the implementation of the constitution and give full scope to the important role of the Constitution as the general norm in governing the country and managing State affairs. As the fundamental law of the State, the Constitution establishes the socialist road with Chinese characteristics, its theoretical system and institutional system, and provides for the fundamental system and fundamental task of the State, the leading core and guiding thought of the State, the basic structure and relevant systems of the State, patriotic united front, the basic strategy for law-based governance of the country, the principle of democratic centralism, the principle of respecting and guaranteeing human rights, etc. Implementing these systems and principles of the Constitution, the system of supervision of the implementation of the constitution is conducive to carrying out national top-level design and strategic layout, according to the Constitution, to promote standardization and establishment of the institutional system for national governance, uplift the authority and effectiveness of national governance capacity.

Good implementation of the Constitution is the inevitable requirement for an effective operation of the institutional system for national governance. The capability of the Party and the State for guaranteeing the implementation of the constitution comprehensively reflects modernization and the law-based development of national governance capacity. General Secretary Xi Jinping pointed out: "The vitality of a system lies in implementation; if a system is not strictly executed, the situation described by the broken windows theory will occur." In order to push forward modernization of national governance capacity, it is necessary to enhance law-based governance of the country and the capacity for governing the country according to the laws, and raise the capacity and level of implementing the Constitution and laws and executing various systems. Full play should be given to the important role of the Constitution in national governance modernization; it is essential to intensify the institutional improvement of the supervision system for the implementation of the constitution , incorporate all State acts into the scope of constitutional supervision, and ensure that national governance modernization proceeds according to the correct direction, nature and path prescribed by the Constitution. The constitutional supervisory system should be improved to prevent and correct various unconstitutional acts, ensure that various kinds of work of State organs do not deviate from the path specified in the Constitution so that national governance is fully under the rule of law.

Third, improving the supervision system for implementation of China's constitution is beneficial to preserving the State system, consolidating the system of government, guaranteeing ethnic solidarity, national unity and territorial integrity. The Constitution is the basic symbol and political mark of a modern country; it is the highest legal basis and the fundamental legal guarantee for national existence and unity, ethnic solidarity and territorial integrity. China's Constitution explicitly states that China is a socialist country under the people's democratic dictatorship led by the working class and based on the alliance of workers and peasants; it also states that the socialist system is China's fundamental system, and the system of a people's congress is China's system of government. As the fundamental law, the Constitution affirms the state system and the system of government and is given the supreme legal authority. Furthermore, in order to safeguard state sovereignty and territorial integrity, the Constitution stipulates the principle of democratic centralism and the relations between the central government and local governments, and affirms the institutional arrangement of the system of regional national autonomy and "One Country, Two Systems". The Constitution is the most fundamental legal form and all-round implementation of the Constitution is the most fundamental institutional guarantee for safeguarding state sovereignty and unity, preserving the basic socialist system, upholding the system of a people's congress and for guaranteeing ethnic solidarity and national territorial integrity. With the supreme legal status and strong legal force, China's current constitution forcefully safeguards national unity, ethnic solidarity and social stability, exerting a far-reaching impact on China's political, economic, cultural and social life. Improving the supervision system for the implementation of the constitution is beneficial to promoting the implementation of the Constitution, preserving the socialist state system and system of government, guaranteeing ethnic solidarity, and safeguarding state sovereignty and territorial security.

In Western countries under the rule of law, regardless of whether there is a judicial review mode (such as the USA), or a constitutional court mode (such as Germany) or a constitutional committee mode (such as France, Finland), the supervision system for the implementation of the constitution plays an important role in solving major conflicts and preserving national unity. In these countries, some political conflicts ultimately evolve into constitutional issues; some social crises are ultimately resolved by the constitutional mechanism; some judicial litigations ultimately develop into constitutional litigations; some legal conflicts are ultimately addressed through constitutional review. In the countries under the rule of law, as a constitutional means, the supervision system for the implementation of the constitution could effectively overcome a crisis of national secession, ethnic conflict crises, political crises of political parties, local independence crises; it might effectively resolve such contradictions and problems as election disputes, a policy's compliance with laws, conflict of laws, whether or not an act complies with the Constitution and it could also be a final remedy for litigations and disputes.

Fourth, improving China's supervision system for the implementation of the constitution helps guarantee the unity and authority of the national legal system, comprehensively promote law-based governance of the country, and turn China into a country under the rule of law. In order to govern the country according to laws, it is necessary to first of all govern the country according to the Constitution. All-round implementation of the Constitution is the primary task and the basic work for comprehensively promoting law-based governance of the country and building a socialist country under the rule of law. It is essential to earnestly work on implementing and supervising the constitution, and develop a more improved legal and institutional system through institutional arrangement and procedural design of constitutional supervision; moreover, it is necessary to ensure consistency between the laws at higher levels and those at lower levels, a high compatibility between special laws and general laws, coordination between procedural laws and substantive laws, a connection between domestic laws and international laws, engagement between judicial interpretations and national legislation, unity between the Party's regulations and national laws, and a correlation between reform decisions and legislative decisions; this guarantees the unity and authority of a national legal system. Improving China's supervision system for the implementation of the constitution is conducive to putting various kinds of work of the state under the rule of law, and improving the system of restriction and supervision of the operation of power, as well as curbing powers within laws and systems; it ensures that power comes with responsibilities; the use of power is subject to supervision; dereliction of duty must be held accountable; violations of laws must be investigated and dealt with. This all ensures that the power granted by the people always serves the people's interests; power is neither exceeded nor abused; dereliction and breach of duty do not occur; nonfeasance is prevented and misconduct is avoided; the country is ruled by laws and the Party is governed according to laws; power is checked by laws and officials are administered according to laws; decisions are made and executed according to laws; arbitrary use and corruption of power is effectively prevented through the supervision system for the implementation of the constitution.

Currently, China's Constitution, the Legislation Law and the Supervision Law contain some principle-oriented provisions for the supervision system for the implementation of the constitution, while these provisions offer the legal basis for improving China's system of constitutional supervision. However, there is no special working body for supervising the implementation of the constitution or for an operable working mechanism and operating procedure during constitutional supervision; the system of supervision of the implementation of the constitution is not effectively operated. In practice, constitutional violations have continued to occur to some extent in some localities and departments. Some leading cadres have manoeuvred personal authority above the Constitution and laws, and have ignored the national legal system and the authority of the Central Committee, abused the powers of the Party and the country, in this way severely damaging the constitutional order. Some leading cadres have defied the Constitution and laws, bent laws for personal gains, abused public power for personal purposes, and trampled on the Constitution. If these unconstitutional acts are not prevented and corrected through the constitutional system and procedure, there will be severe damage to the authority of the Constitution and the credibility of State acts will be affected. Further improving the system of supervision of the implementation of the constitution and giving full play to the function of supervising the implementation of the constitution is the key to promoting law-based governance of the country in an all-round way; this is "the last defensive line" for preserving the authority of the Constitution and is the most effective means for guaranteeing the comprehensive implementation of the Constitution. As shown by the proven facts, correcting one unconstitutional act is more effective than publicizing the Constitution one hundred times, and is more beneficial to the leading cadres at various levels in developing a constitutional line of thought and in upholding the authority of the Constitution. If the supervision system for the implementation of the constitution as a key link is unavailable or weakened, the Constitution will be nothing but a "straw man" without authority and may be reduced to a mere scrap of paper; furthermore, the foundation for law-based governance of the country will be eroded, and the rule of law will be like a tree without roots and water without a source from the perspective of unity and authority.

Fifth, improving China's supervision system for the implementation of the constitution is conducive to building a national constitutional order, achieving social equity and justice, and maintaining the enduring stability of the Party and the country. The constitutional order is a state of orderly political, economic and social life in the country, which is based on the design, implementation and observance of the Constitution; it is the greatest, beneficial concentration of the political, economic and social order as well as the security of the country. The Constitution helps build a consensus of the fundamental values in the society; it is the fundamental basis for governing the country and handling the affairs of State; it is the legal guarantee for maintaining social equity and justice. In China, the scope of bodies responsible for implementing the Constitution is very wide; its implementation modes are diverse; State organs, the armed forces and social groups implement the Constitution within the scope of their respective functions and powers to jointly build a national constitutional order.

General Secretary Xi Jinping pointed out, "comprehensively promoting law-based governance of the country is the fundamental requirement for addressing a number of major issues for the causes of the Party and the country, emancipating and boosting social vitality, promoting social equity and justice, maintaining social harmony and stability, ensuring the prolonged stability of the Party and the country."① In order to comprehensively promote law-based governance of the

① Xi Jinping, "Explanatory Notes for the *Decision of the Central Committee of the Communist Party of China on Some Major Issues Concerning Comprehensively Promoting Law-based Governance of the Country*".

country, it is necessary to first of all push forward the implementation of the constitution in an all-round way and ensure the effective implementation of the constitution. As China's supervision system for the implementation of the constitution is the last means for maintaining a national constitutional order, improvement of this system of supervision helps coordinate various mechanisms of constitutional implementation in order to build a unified, harmonious constitutional order, preserve social equity and justice, and maintain a lasting stability of the Party and the country.

Sixth, improving China's supervision system for the implementation of the constitution helps, at the theoretical and institutional level, make a fundamental differentiation from the Western mode of constitutional democracy, and boost the confidence of the whole Party, army and all of the people in China's road, theory and system. China's Constitution establishes the socialist road with Chinese characteristics, its theoretical and institutional system, and shapes the socialist constitutional system with Chinese characteristics which centers on governing the country and managing the affairs of State according to the Constitution ("China's constitutional system"). There are differences between China's constitutional system and the Western mode of constitutional democracy With respect to the nature of class, the social system, constitutional principles, power holding, political systems, political party systems, power distribution and operational mechanism. China's Constitution is a good constitution consistent with national conditions, and with the requirements of the reality and with the development of the era ; it is a good constitution which fully reflects the common will of the people, fully guarantees the democratic rights of the people, and adequately safeguards the fundamental interests of the people; it is a good constitution which promotes national development and progress, and ensures that the people are able to create a happy life and the Chinese nation can achieve great rejuvenation. China's constitutional system stresses the unity of the State system — people's democratic dictatorship — and the system of government —the system of a people's congress; it underlines the unity of the Party's leadership, the people being masters of the country and law-based governance of the country; it upholds the socialist road with Chinese characteristics and its theories, and improves the socialist system with Chinese characteristics, thus it is a good constitution. However, there is no well-enhanced, effective supervision system for the implementation of the constitution; some unconstitutional acts including unconstitutional reforms and unconstitutional use of power cannot be publicly, appropriately redressed through constitutional channels; some basic spirits, principles, requirements and rights prescribed by the Constitution cannot be comprehensively and deeply carried out, so it is not easy for the general public to recognize the advantages and characteristics of China's Constitution and constitutional system, nor perfectly understand the socialist road with Chinese characteristics, its theories, institutional significance and connotations established by the Constitution; it is difficult to build a value consensus throughout the society, and foster the constitutional belief with confidence in China's road, theory and system. It is necessary to improve China's system of supervision of the implementation of the constitution and expound the socialist theories and systems with Chinese characteristics established by the Constitution in specific matters and cases, because this helps uphold the socialist constitutional system with Chinese characteristics, clarify the essential difference between China's constitutional road and the Western mode of constitutional democracy, and boost the confidence of the whole Party, army and the whole people in China's road, theory and system.

4.3 Basic principles for Building and Improving the Supervison System for the Implementation of China's Constitution

In essence, China's constitutional system is different from the Western mode of constitutional democracy. With respect to improvement of China's system of supervision of the implementation of the constitution, China should copy neither the mode of constitutional democracy of Western capitalist countries, nor the constitutional democratic system of other socialist countries; instead, China should proceed from its national conditions and reality and draw upon the beneficial experience of the supervision of constitutional implementation in foreign countries, and carry out the institutional design within the framework of China's Constitution. The following several basic principles should be upheld in order to improve China's supervision system for the implementation of the constitution.

First, the socialist road towards supervision of the implementation of the constitution with Chinese characteristics should be followed, while the Western constitutional review system should not be adopted. Improving China's supervision system for the implementation of the constitution is a profound reform of the political system, and represents the self-improvement, self-adaptation and self-development of China's constitutional system. It is necessary to improve the design of relevant systems and procedures under the Party's leadership and under the basic principles and basic institutional framework established by China's Constitution, while it is absolutely impossible to copy the mode of constitutional review of Western countries, and adopt the mode of judicial review conducted by courts under the tripartite political system in the USA. China's system of supervision of the implementation of the constitution must be based on the fundamental political system — the system of a people's congress — with full scope given to the leading role of the people's congresses and their standing committees in the supervision of the implementation of the constitution.

Second, the leadership of the Communist Party in the supervision of the implementation of the constitution must be upheld, while the constitutional review system under the Western multi-party system must not be adopted. Upholding the Party's leadership is the basic principle prescribed by China's Constitution and it is also the most fundamental political guarantee for comprehensive implementation of the Constitution. One basic experience since the promulgation and implementation of the current constitution is that full play should be given to the core leading role in the implementation of the constitution, and various departments and localities should be mobilized as a whole, and the implementation of the constitution should be promoted in a coordinated and comprehensive way. As shown by bitter lessons from the demise of the Soviet Union and the downfall of the Communist Party of the Soviet Union, the implementation of the constitution was not led by that party, it was caught in the institutional trap of copying Western constitutional democracy so that disruptive mistakes on fundamental issues were made.

The Western system of constitutional review is built on the premise of a two-party system or a multi-party system — its functional design stresses the guarantee of democratic elections, multi-party competition and rotation of power, and its institutional design emphasizes party politics, wrestling between or among political parties, checks and balances, so mutual entanglement and restriction and standoffs easily occur in constitutional supervision. In order to further improve the supervision system for the implementation of the constitution under which the Communist Party of China is solely in power and multiple parties cooperate and participate in governance, overall coordination must be strengthened under the Party's leadership and "constitutional impasse", or even "constitutional crisis", must be absolutely avoided. Upholding and guaranteeing the Party's leadership in supervising the implementation of the constitution is the inevitable requirement for governance of the country conducted by the Communist Party of China according to the Constitution and the safeguarding of the Constitution's authority; this is also the most distinctive feature and the greatest advantage of China's supervision of the implementation of the constitution. Subject to the Party's leadership and the constitutional framework, the Party governs the country and manages the affairs of State, grasps the overall situation and coordinates various parties to ensure that the people's congress, government, political consultative conference, adjudication and procuratorial organs perform their functions and carry out their work according to the laws and the Party's constitution; moreover, the Party leads the people in making and implementing the Constitution and laws, and conducts activities according to the Constitution and laws; only in this way can the mechanisms of the implementation of the constitution in various departments and different fields be effectively integrated to comprehensively supervise the implementation of the constitution and practically uphold the authority of the Constitution.

Third, the system of a people's congress must be maintained, while the constitutional review system under the Western tripartite political system and two-chamber system should not be adopted. Under the system of a people's congress, the principle of democratic centralism is followed; unicameralism is practiced; the State Council, the Supreme People's Court and the Supreme People's Procuratorate are created by the people's congress to which they are responsible and by which they are supervised. This is the fundamental difference between China's supervision system for the implementation of the constitution and the constitutional review system based on the tripartite political system and the two-chamber system in Western countries. In order to intensify efforts to improve China's supervision system for the implementation of the constitution, it is necessary to promote the development of relevant systems and mechanisms under the system of a people's congress; moreover, it is necessary not to deviate from or break the constitutional framework for the system of a people's congress at any time. China's Constitution explicitly grants constitutional supervisory power to the National People's Congress and its Standing Committee. The improvement of the supervision system for the implementation of the constitution must be adapted to the functional division, institutional practice and working mechanism of the National People's Congress and its Standing Committee; such improvement must match the constitutional principles and arrangements for the system of a people's congress; it must be consistent with the basic principles by which the Party plays the leading role, and the people are the masters of the country and the country is ruled by laws; the improvement must reduce the impact on the existing political habits and legal order as much as possible, and preserve the stability and authority of the system of a people's congress to the greatest extent.

Fourth, national unity, ethnic solidarity and the unity of rule of law must be upheld, while the system of constitutional review under the federal system and decentralization system in the Western countries must not be adopted. China is a multinational, permanently unitary country under the unitary system. The improvement of the supervision system for the implementation of the constitution must be conducive to upholding national unity, promoting ethnic solidarity and guaranteeing the unity of the rule of law. In the Western federal countries, one important function of the system of constitutional review consists of settling the constitutional disputes between the federation and various parts to preserve the integrity of the federal countries. The functional orientation of the supervision system for the implementation of the constitution under the unitary system in China is different from the constitutional review mode under a federal system. China's supervision of the implementation of the constitution is exercised by giving full scope to the initiative and enthusiasm of local authorities under the unified leadership of the Central Committee, and by fully ensuring that local organs of the State (especially in ethnic regional autonomous areas and special administrative regions) exercise their powers and perform their duties to conduct governance according to the Constitution and laws. In order to further improve the system of supervision of the implementation of the constitution, it is necessary to maintain the unity of a socialist rule of law, and the stability of the constitutional order, preserve national unity and ethnic solidarity, adopt this system to effectively avoid national secession and disintegration, and prevent and resolve ethnic contradictions and conflicts.

Fifth, the first priority should be given to prevention, guidance and coordination in order to avoid the facts and cases of constitutional violations. The constitutional review system in Western countries is based on a tripartite political system and a multi-party system; such a system stresses the separation of powers, checks and balances, post supervision; as a result, under such a system, political parties and powers often vie with each other and refuse to give ground, causing constitutional impasse, greatly affecting the capacity of the State and the stability of the constitutional order. China's supervision system for the implementation of the constitution is based on three cornerstones — the Party's leadership, the system of a people's congress and the system of democratic centralism; under this system, it is necessary to focus on prevention, guidance and coordination, and actively carry out prevention and supervision beforehand, nip constitutional violations in the bud, handle constitutional violations at the initial stage, and adopt a feasible supervision system for the implementation of the constitution in order to prevent the facts and cases of constitutional violations. Under China's supervision system for the implementation of the constitution, active prevention and supervision beforehand is a normal state, while post correction of constitutional violations and unconstitutional acts is a standby legal means used only when necessary or compelled to take action, In general, prevention and supervision against constitutional violations beforehand is a normal state, while post correction of constitutional violations is a standby constitutional means which is not or seldomly used.

4.4 Functional Positioning of the Supervision System for the Implementation of China's Constitution

The Constitution serves as the general constitution for administering the affairs of State well and ensuring national security. The Constitution is the fundamental legal basis for governing the country and managing State affairs. For the improvement of China's system of supervision of the implementation of the constitution, the functions of this system should be brought into play regarding the following several aspects.

4.4.1 Declaration

As the fundamental law, China's Constitution establishes the socialist system as the fundamental system of the country, affirms the basic political, economic, cultural and social system of the country, as well as the basic rights and obligations of its citizens. A series of affirmations in China's Constitution are public declarations made to the whole world in the form of the fundamental law of the country, and explicit declarations made to the people across the country in the form of the general constitution for administering the affairs of State well and for ensuring national security. The declaration function of the Constitution needs to be materialized through the system of constitutional supervision. The improvement of the system of constitutional supervision is conducive to vividly presenting, in a concrete constitutional form, the fundamental system and value ideas prescribed by the Constitution, and enhancing the sense of the Constitution in the whole society; it helps build a value consensus in the society, shape mainstream social ideology, instill the socialist core values prescribed by the Constitution in the people, and foster a society-wide confidence in the road, theory and system based on the Constitution.

4.4.2 Guidance

The Constitution serves as the fundamental legal basis for governing the country and managing the affairs of State. The Constitution plays an overarching role in national governance. China's Constitution establishes the guiding thoughts and the fundamental tasks of the State; the system of constitutional supervision can make these basic philosophies and goals concrete, it gives scope to the standardizing role of the Constitution, and the philosophies and goals established by the Constitution are adopted to lead national governance so that national governance falls completely under the rule of law. The system of constitutional supervision is able to guide the efforts in comprehensively coordinating the legislation, law enforcement and judicial processes and different State organs to jointly promote all-round implementation of the strategy for a law-based governance of the country. Constitutional supervision is a self-improvement mechanism in China's Constitution and legal system; as the legal system is continuously optimized on the basis of the Constitution, on the one hand, this helps guide improvement and development of the legal system with Chinese characteristics; on the other hand, it is conducive to implementing the principle that "major reforms must be based on laws" and on leading efforts to intensify the reforms and build a moderately prosperous society in an all-round way.

4.4.3 Governance

The most fundamental aspect of national governance is constitutional governance, while the most important aspect of the modernization of national governance is the modernization of the supervision of the implementation of the constitution. Internationally, constitutional supervision is the important means for national governance. In the modern Western modern countries under the rule of law, the system of constitutional supervision is widely established, showing a high capacity of national governance. In China, as the important institutional channel for carrying out the will of the Party and the people, the system of constitutional supervision is beneficial to the Party in controlling the key link for achieving the modernization of national governance, and comprehensively enhancing the capacity for governing the country and managing the affairs of State. With the improvement of the system of constitutional supervision, the National People's Congress and its Standing Committee follow the legal procedure to timely correct the unconstitutional acts, and interpret the constitutional norms so that the Party's positions on relevant issues can be elevated in due time to State will through legal procedure. As long as the Party Central Committee controls the key link — the system of constitutional supervision -- and carries out the Central Committee's intentions regarding decisions in dealing with constitutional issues, the sanctity of the Constitution can be upheld, the unity of the legal system can be preserved and the decisions of the Central Committee can be smoothly implemented; furthermore, the Central Committee can shift its focus from controlling the State organs, groups and organizations at the middle and low levels to studying and pushing forward the strategies for comprehensively building a moderately prosperous society, intensifying reforms, governing the country according to laws, and strengthening party self-discipline, thus practically giving play to the core leading role of the Party in the key fields involving governance of the country and management of the affairs of State.

4.4.4 Legitimacy

The Constitution is the basis for the legitimacy of the legal system. As a legal judgment regarding State acts is made according to the Constitution, State acts can become legitimate. As judgment regarding constitutional compliance about legal norms is made, their legitimacy at the constitutional level can be directly strengthened. Even if there is a judgment regarding constitutional violation, the adoption of and treatment based on legal techniques can also turn specific legal norms or State acts into legitimate ones. Constitutional supervision does not merely identify laws and regulations as unconstitutional and invalid; as the intrinsic requirement for a mechanism for guaranteeing the implementation of the constitution, another important function of constitutional supervision is that constitutional supervision enables the constitutional legitimacy of State acts so as to foster the authority and credibility of those acts.

4.4.5 Supervision

Constitutional supervision is the most important and most fundamental supervision in the national system of supervision, and it is the general supervision over governance of the country and management of the affairs of State. As part of the national system of supervision, constitutional supervision plays an important role in supervising the operation of State power according to the laws. As the highest national legal supervision, constitutional supervision has the highest legal validity over all State organs, social groups and the armed forces. With the improvement of the system of supervision of the implementation of the constitution, the highest commanding function of the Constitution can be brought into play and various mechanisms of supervision can be fully integrated, thus building a solid institutional means for the State to supervise and check powers and ensuring that all State powers are operated according to the Constitution and laws.

4.5 Establishing and Improving the Top-level Design of the Supervision System for the Implementation of China's Constitution

When completely revising the Constitution in 1982, the Constitution Revision Committee once considered the establishment of a special body for constitutional supervision, and the Secretariat conducted a special study on this issue. In 1983, 30 deputies to the National People's Congress, including Wang Shuwen, once jointly submitted a proposal to the 6th National People's Congress to suggest that a Constitution Committee should be set up. At that time, the working personnel at the Secretariat of the Constitution Revision Committee designed four plans for the mechanism of constitutional supervision.①

Plan One:

The following two articles should be added to Section One of

① Liu Songshan, "1981: Shaped but Aborted Design of Constitution Committee", *Tribune of Political Science and Law*, 2010 (5).

Chapter Two:

Article ** The Constitution Committee of the National People's Congress is the organ of the National People's Congress for hearing major constitutional violations.

The Constitution Committee of the National People's Congress consists of 9-13 members elected by the National People's Congress, and their term is the same as that of each National People's Congress.

The Constitution Committee of the National People's Congress is responsible for and reports to the National People's Congress.

Article ** The Constitution Committee of the National People's Congress exercises the following functions and powers:

(1) It may submit the laws or decrees which contravene the Constitution to the National People's Congress or to the Standing Committee of the National People's Congress for reconsideration;

(2) It has the power to decide on whether or not administrative regulations and local regulations contravene the Constitution;

(3) It has the power to review and deal with major unconstitutional acts of the central State organs and leaders of the central State organs.

Plan Two:

The following article should be added to Section Two of Chapter Two:

Article ** The Constitution Committee is established within the Standing Committee of the National People's Congress. The Constitution Committee assists the Standing Committee of the National People's Congress in supervising the implementation of the Constitution. The Constitution Committee submits a report and handling opinions regarding the unconstitutional laws, decrees, other unconstitutional regulations and the unconstitutional acts of the central State organs and leaders of the central State organs to the Standing Committee of the National People's Congress.

Plan Three:

The following article should be added to Section Seven of Chapter Two:

Article ** The Supreme People's Procuratorate exercises the power to supervise whether or not laws, decrees, other regulations, the acts of leaders of state organs and the central State organs comply with the

Constitution.

Plan Four:

The article concerning incorporation of the Constitution Committee as a special committee (permanent committee) into the National People's Congress and the Standing Committee of the National People's Congress should be added to Section One of Chapter One:

Article ** The National People's Congress establishes the Constitution Committee, the Ethnic Affairs Committee, the Planned Budget Committee and other special committees which need to be established. Special committees are under the leadership of the Standing Committee of the National People's Congress when the National People's Congress is not in session.

Among the above four plans, the first and second plans involve the design of the Constitution Committee, while the third plan actually grants the Supreme People's Procuratorate with the power to exercise constitutional supervision, and the fourth plan establishes a special committee — the Constitution & Law Committee under the National People's Congress. When the Constitution was revised in 1993, as some local authorities and organizations proposed to add a provision that "the Constitutional Supervisory Committee be established within the National People's Congress" to Article 70 of the Constitution, the Party Central Committee pointed out in the *Supplementary Suggestions Concerning the Revision of Part of the Constitution*, "according to Article 70 of the Constitution, the National People's Congress may establish a special constitutional supervisory committee, and the Constitution might not incorporate a provision in this regard." In two subsequent constitutional revisions, many experts and scholars proposed establishing the Constitution Committee. At present, with respect to the establishment of a special constitutional supervisory body under the National People's Congress, in-depth theoretical research has been conducted, and such a body is necessary for comprehensively governing the country according to laws, and is feasible in constitutional and legal practice, so the time is ripe for establishing a special socialist constitutional supervisory body with Chinese characteristics.

4.5.1 Implementation plan for establishing a constitutional supervisory body

The establishment of a constitutional supervisory body must be initiated as soon as possible under the leadership of the Party Central Committee in a coordinated way according to the unified arrangement. Presently, consideration may be given to establishing a temporary coordinating body for constitutional supervision at the central level, which may be led and arranged in coordination with comprehensive law-based governance of the country, and is tentatively named "the Central Leading Group for Promoting the Implementation of the Constitution and Law-based Governance of the Country". With regard to the supervision of the implementation of the constitution, it mainly coordinates relevant central departments and State organs in an all-round way, and studies major theoretical and practical issues concerning the implementation of the constitution and its supervision, and promotes improvement of the mechanism of supervision of the implementation of the constitution in a coordinated way.

Under the unified leadership of the Party Central Committee, different plans may be considered and executed step by step to gradually improve the system and mechanism of supervision of the implementation of the constitution.

The first plan is that a special working body for supervision of the implementation of the constitution is established within the Standing Committee of the National People's Congress, which could be named "Constitutional Supervision Committee" put forward by the Party Central Committee in the *Supplementary Suggestions Concerning the Revision of Part of the Constitution*. The newly-established Constitutional Supervision Committee may share the same working place with the Commission of Legislative Affairs of the Standing Committee of the National People's Congress and may have an office as a working body for routine work. It is mainly responsible for studying and dealing with the laws, regulations and local regulations, in the current legal system, that contravene the Constitution. Its working mechanism may be connected to the laws and regulations filing review mechanism. If constitutional violations are found, they are opportunely delivered according to respective functions and powers to relevant organs for studying and handling. The above plan has a minimal impact on the current system and working mechanism of the people's congress and can be executed with relatively low costs and little resistance.

The second plan is that when the time is ripe and where necessary, a constitutional supervisory body is established within the National People's Congress. Establishment of a constitutional supervisory body under the Standing Committee is only a transitional plan for improving the system of constitutional supervision and is makeshift. According to Article 62 of the Constitution, the National People's Congress has the power to supervise the implementation of the constitution. In order to strengthen supervision over the implementation of the constitution, a special constitutional supervisory body in parallel with other special committees may be established according to the decision made by the National People's Congress. As a special committee established by the highest organ of State power is responsible for supervising the implementation of the constitution, this is beneficial to reflecting the democracy of constitutional supervision and making constitutional supervision more special, professional and authoritative. Meanwhile, the functions of relevant special committees should be integrated to address the overlap of function and power; for example, the Constitutional Supervision Committee may have functions and powers which overlap those of the Law Committee, the Committee for Internal & Judicial Affairs and other special committees in legal compliance review and legal supervision, thus the scope of respective functions and powers should be clarified and the constitutional issues should be rationally differentiated from general legal issues to engage in collaboration based on explicit division of work to jointly promote supervision over the constitution and law enforcement.

The third plan is that, where necessary in the future, reference is made to the mode of the Central Military Committee to establish the Constitutional Supervision Committee which is under the dual leadership of the Party Central Committee and the National People's Congress and is in parallel with the Standing Committee of the National People's Congress so as to comprehensively strengthen the intensity and function of governance of the country conducted by the Party according to the

Constitution, and enhance the capability of the State for governance based on the Constitution and the quality of its governance. In time of peace, at a new historical starting point, the Party has fully transformed from a revolutionary political party to a governing party, and attaches greater importance to the important roles of the Constitution and the rule of law, thus it is necessary to enhance the system of constitutional supervision as the general means for the Party to govern the country, manage state affairs and comprehensively promote law-based governance of the country. The implementation of the constitution should be intensified to deepen the governance of the Party, the country and the army in an all-round way, and the constitutional supervision should be strengthened to comprehensively reinforce the Party's leadership, and the governance of the country and the society.

4.5.2 Main functions of the constitutional supervisory body

Specifically, the constitutional supervisory body mainly performs the following functions:

(1) Drafts the constitutional interpretation, submits it to the National People's Congress or to its Standing Committee for solicitation of public opinions, deliberation and voting;

(2) Puts forward review opinions concerning constitutional violations and submits them to the National People's Congress and to its Standing Committee for discussion;

(3) Conducts a filing review of the socialist legal system with Chinese characteristics;

(4) Puts forward deliberation opinions concerning other constitutional proposals delivered by the presidium of the National People's Congress or its Standing Committee;

(5) Regularly summarizes and evaluates the implementation of the constitution and reports it to the Standing Committee;

(6) Works with relevant organs of the governing party to review the part of the Party's regulations which overlaps the national laws for constitutional compliance;

(7) Puts forward review opinions concerning the treaties and important agreements between China and foreign countries for

constitutional and legal compliance in China;

(8) Puts forward review opinions concerning the necessity and constitutional compliance of the decision about a state of emergency made by the State or particular provinces, autonomous regions, municipalities directly under the Central Government;

(9) Conducts surveys and research on the constitutional issues raised by particular local authorities, groups, parties or nationalities, and reports them to the National People's Congress or its Standing Committee;

(10) Performs other matters entrusted by the National People's Congress or its Standing Committee.

4.5.3 Working principles regarding the constitutional supervisory body

China's constitutional supervisory body is a special body for supervising comprehensive implementation of the Constitution, and its functions and powers are defined under the following four principles, thus it is different from the separation of powers, checks and balances under the Western constitutional democratic mode. In China, constitutional supervision should follow the following principles:

First, prevention is stressed, supplemented by post correction. Under the socialist constitutional supervision system, restriction, check and balance should not be adopted, instead, emphasis should be placed on beforehand prevention, while post correction of constitutional violations only serves as a supplementary means. This helps, at source, reduce constitutional violations and constitutional disputes, and nip constitutional violations in the bud as far as possible rather than make post correction of constitutional violations.

Second, constitutionality judgment is stressed, supplemented by unconstitutionality judgment. As shown by the systems of constitutional supervision in different countries around the world, constitutionality judgments make up the majority, while there are few unconstitutionality judgments. The principle of absolute necessity should be followed for unconstitutionality judgment in China's constitutional supervision — if there is no sufficient necessity, unconstitutionality judgments should be reduced as much as possible, and only when there is absolute necessity, should an unconstitutionality judgment be made.

Third, legal issues are stressed, supplemented by political issues. Constitutional supervision is a working mechanism for addressing legal issues and resolving legal disputes, thus generally political issues are not addressed. Constitutional supervision should be exercised by dodging political issues; in particular, political issues concerning such fields as foreign affairs, the military and national defense should not be included in the procedure of constitutional supervision.

Fourth, passive review is stressed, supplemented by active review. In order to preserve the existing pattern of State power as far as possible, constitutional supervision should be based on the principle of "no trial without complaint" — passive review should prevail, while active review is an exception.

5. Measures and Suggestions for Improving China's Filing Review System

According to the Constitution, the Legislation Law and the Supervision Law, specific state organs, enterprises, public organizations and citizens may make a review request or suggestion to the National People's Congress for reviewing whether specific legal norms, including administrative regulations, local regulations, regulations on the exercise of autonomy and separate regulations, rules, judicial interpretations, contravene the laws at higher levels. This system is designed to improve the existing legal system and can be deemed an inherent mechanism for optimization in the socialist legal system with Chinese characteristics. At the new developmental stage of the socialist legal system with Chinese characteristics, this system is of great significance for implementing the basic strategy for law-based governance of the country in a deep-going way.

5.1 Mechanism for Initiating Filing Review

The similarity in laws and regulations of the filing review system between China and foreign countries is the system for constitutional review of laws and regulations. The review systems of different countries can be divided into centralized review and decentralized review by the review mode; they can be divided into judicial organ review, special organ review and public opinion organ review by the review organ.

However, the review method broadly includes abstract review and concrete review, regardless of the review system. The former does take the case as a precondition and merely involves a review on whether or not abstract laws and regulations comply with the laws at higher levels. The latter involves a review on whether or not specific laws and regulations comply with the laws at higher levels in a specific case. Both methods have advantages and disadvantages, so both methods can be adopted in most cases in the practice of various countries.

China's current filing review system mainly works at the level of internal operation and there is no effective feedback and response mechanism for public participation. If a public participation mechanism is introduced to China's filing review system, reference may be made to relevant mechanisms concerning feedback and response to the applications from the general public in foreign review systems to gradually improve China's system. The following three main issues need to be considered at different stages:

First, once an extensive public participation mechanism is introduced, how does the review organ screen and identify the applications filed by a large number of people or other statutory bodies? This is the first issue for the filing review organ. In this regard, reference may be made to foreign institutional practice by establishing necessary thresholds — requirements for review initiation — to exclude the applications inconsistent with legal requirements from the legal procedure. It is similar to the case filing system of courts. Thresholds vary with different modes of review system, providing a reference for improving China's relevant systems.

Second, which applications and appeals can enter the review procedure? How to review whether or not relevant laws contravene the laws at higher levels? Which criteria and legal methods are adopted for review? In this respect, reference may be made to the review criteria and methods extensively adopted by foreign review organs; for example, which review criterion (strict or loose criterion) should be adopted in light of different circumstances? How can the review methods be applied based on legislative facts? How can legislative inactions be handled?

Finally, how can the legal norms which do not comply with the laws at higher levels as shown by review be handled? Foreign systems place more emphasis on post review and legal judgment. China's filing review system was once criticized as a system under which filing is made but no review is conducted, and no conclusion is drawn even if review is conducted. In order to further respond to relevant applications, it is necessary to further handle the laws and regulations which contravene the Constitution and the laws at higher levels; for example, how can their validity be affirmed? Are the administrative acts committed or judicial decisions made according to these laws and regulations in the past still valid? These issues need to be carefully addressed.

5.2 Feedback and Response Mechanism for Filing Review

For China's current review system, there is an urgent need to clarify how to make feedback and response to the request or suggestion from the applicant. Undeniably, China's filing review system was established late; relevant experience is insufficient; there is less interaction among relevant legal bodies; however, the improvement of any system entails a process; introduction of the public participation mechanism and improvement of China's filing review system should be based on continuous experimentation and orderly advancement, and it cannot be accomplished overnight. Given the current legal development and current situation of the filing review system in China, first, it is necessary to establish an open mechanism to gradually publicize the number of filed laws and regulations, the number of review suggestions and handling information. Second, some applications consistent with requirements are chosen to conduct reviews, developing legal opinions, and making public feedback. Third, some legal norms consistent with the laws at higher levels should be affirmed for legal compliance so as to dispel the doubts among the people from all walks of life, and preserve the authority of laws. Finally, it is necessary to gradually expand the participation channels to arouse the enthusiasm of the general public for participation, solicit pubic opinions, pool the wisdom of the people, and continuously improve the socialist legal system with Chinese characteristics.

5.3 Mechanism for the Classified Handling of Laws and Regulations

According to Article 90 of the Legislation Law, the applicants are classified into the following three categories: the first category covers the organs which can make a review request according to laws (the State Council, the Military Committee, the Supreme People's Court, the Supreme People's Procuratorate, the provincial people's congresses); the second category includes the general bodies and social organizations which can make a review suggestion according to laws (State organs, social groups, enterprises and public institutions); the third category involves the citizens. The above different review applicants should be separately dealt with. With respect to the first category of applicants, according to the Legislation Law, it is explicit — the working body of the Standing Committee delivers their requests to special relevant committees for reviewing and expressing opinions. When the second category and the third category of applicants put forward review suggestions, the key lies in how to judge "where necessary" specified in Article 90 of the Legislation Law. How should this be addressed? Certain criteria are required. In foreign countries, especially those countries under a system of common law, these criteria are often cumulatively generated in practice and specific cases. The practical legal development in the countries under a system of continental law also shows a similar trend. China may make reference to the relatively ripe experience in these countries to develop its own criteria for judgment.

5.4 Functional Positioning of the Filing Review System

China's filing review system may offer a legal channel for the general public to participate in improving and developing the legal system. In fact, such a system may also help provide civic rights relief and settle disputes. At present, with the introduction of the civic participation and filing review mechanism, two other important functions, which can be realized by this kind of system, except the participation channel, should also be considered.

5.4.1 Civic participation

As the filing review system offers the way and channel for civic participation, it is necessary to consider the scope and extent of the civic participation. Civic participation is only a part of filing review and mainly occurs in the procedure of the review initiation. Therefore such participation cannot exceed the necessary limit. The following several issues need to be studied:

First, are participants restricted to the parties involved in legal interests? Is a third party standing permitted? In foreign countries, certain restrictions are generally imposed on their qualification in the review procedure so that participants are not too general. Chinese laws have no restrictions on such a qualification. Practical operations need to be studied.

Second, what is the difference between such civic participation and the civic participation in the legislation procedure? In the legislation procedure, pubic opinions are solicited to build a consensus, thus the scope and extent of civic participation should be maximized as much as possible. However, whether the same principle should be followed in the filing review procedure deserves thinking and research. One preliminary conclusion is that the filing review procedure is different from the general legislation procedure and the civic participation in the filing review procedure should not be maximized to the greatest extent. The organ of power should remain sober-minded and civic participation should be introduced in a gradual and orderly way according to laws.

Third, the relationship between civic participation and information disclosure is involved. The general information disclosure law has not yet been enacted in China, while the *Information Disclosure Regulations* issued by the State Council are only applicable to administrative organs. No laws are available for governing how to make information disclosure in the filing review procedure. However, the precondition for introducing civic participation is the disclosure of various kinds of information, so a relevant supporting disclosure system is necessary in order to provide a guarantee.

5.4.2 Right of relief

In China, citizens can participate in state affairs through many channels.

In particular, with continuous legal development and improvement, many participation channels have been placed under the rule of law. Besides civic morals, one very important cause for the enthusiasm of high participation is the realization of their legitimate rights; for example, as shown by the evolution and development of China's complaint-related visit and letter system, one important factor affecting citizens' enthusiasm for participation is the appeal for the right of relief. Initially, as the channel for the people to lodge complaints, put forward suggestions and opinions was through letters and visits, the complaint-related visit and letter system mainly helped achieve civic participation. However, in practice, this system has become a channel for the ordinary citizens to seek the right of relief. Given the original intention and functional orientation of the institutional design, the complaint-related visit and letter system has been distorted and alienated to some extent in reality. Therefore, when civic participation is introduced during the implementation of the filing review system, it is necessary to take the implementation of the complaint-related visit and letter system as a mirror; where necessary, overall considerations may be given and coordinated implementation may be conducted by improving the complaint-related visit and letter system of the people's congress.

When it comes to foreign systems, the review organs in various countries often carry out a systematic review of laws and regulations and the legal systems are unified; furthermore, a relief channel is provided for the rights of participants. According to functional orientation and classification of the review system by Western scholars, the review system under the American model lies in guaranteeing personal rights, so it is called the review under the private rights model; the value orientation of the constitutional review under the continental European mode is different from the American private rights guarantee function, thus it is called special function model or constitutional guarantee model, and its main function consists of guaranteeing the implementation of the constitution and the unity of the legal system.[①] Of course, the above

① Henry Monaghan, "Constitutional Adjudication: The Who and When", 82 *Yale Law Journal* 1365 (1973); (Japan) Nobuyoshi Ashibe, Modern Development of Constitutional Litigation, Yuhikaku Publishing, 1982, pp.4-6.

two value orientations are not incompatible — if a right is deemed an objective legal norm, a certain degree of integration between the two values — the guarantee of rights and the realization of the legal order can also be achieved. Therefore, the institutional trend in the world is the concurrent emphasis on both value orientations.

5.4.3 Dispute settlement

According to the foreign constitutional theory, a reviewing organ for laws and regulations is neither a judicial organ nor a legislative organ in a broad sense; instead, it is an independent body which falls outside the category of traditional State power and is responsible for guaranteeing the unity of the legal system and the comprehensive implementation of a constitution.[①] Thanks to this aloof constitutional status, it performs an important function of dispute settlement in legal practice.

Under China's system with the National People's Congress as the highest organ of supreme power, the interpretation made by the National People's Congress with respect to the applicability of some specific laws has gone beyond the traditional legislative functional orientation and it has a certain function of dispute settlement. Of course, this function is not pure since the pure dispute settlement function means that a judgment regarding the key points of disputes submitted for settlement should be made and the organ of power must aim at settling private rights disputes by addressing the issues, thus a legal judgment should be restricted to disputes over particular cases, while other legal issues unrelated to disputes should not be addressed.

In China's legal practice, as a legal organ of interpretation, the National People's Congress once performed an important function of dispute settlement; for example, in criminal judicial practice, with respect to how to consider the personnel of grass-roots organizations including villagers' committees as "other personnel engaged in public affairs" by judging the type of their work, the interpretation of the adjudication of the Supreme People's Court was not consistent with

① Norman Dorsen, Michel Rosenfeld, Andras Sajo, Susanne Baer, "Comparative Constitutionalism: Cases and Materials", West Group, 2003, p.120.

the procuratorial interpretation of the Supreme People's Procuratorate, causing contradictions and conflicts between criminal charges and court judgment. In order to solve this problem, the Commission of Legislative Affairs of the National People's Congress worked out a relevant legislative interpretation and submitted it to the Standing Committee of the National People's Congress. On April 29, 2000, the *Interpretation of the Second Paragraph of Article 93 of the Criminal Law of the People's Republic of China* was passed in the 15th Session of the Standing Committee of the 9th National People's Congress, which explicitly states that only when the personnel of grass-roots organizations including villagers committees assist the people's government in carrying out specific administrative management work can they be considered as "other personnel engaged in public affairs", thus solving the above problem.①

Article 32 of the Supervision Law reads: "When the State Council, the Central Military Committee, and the Standing Committees of the People's Congresses of provinces, autonomous regions and municipalities directly under the Central Government believe that the interpretations made by the Supreme People's Court and the Supreme People's Procuratorate with respect to specific governing laws contravene legal provisions, and the Supreme People's Court and the Supreme People's Procuratorate believe that the interpretation made by the other party with respect to specific governing laws contravenes legal provisions, they may make a written review request to the Standing Committee of the People's Congress; the working body of the Standing Committee must deliver it to the relevant special committee for reviewing and expressing an opinion. When other State organs, social groups, enterprises, public institutions and citizens not enumerated above believe that the interpretations made by the Supreme People's Court and the Supreme People's Procuratorate with respect to specific governing laws contravene legal provisions, they may make a written review suggestion to the Standing Committee of the People's Congress; the working body of the Standing Committee must conduct a study, and where necessary, deliver it to the relevant

---

① Zhao Bingzhi, Shi Yanan, "Brief Discussion about the Legislative Interpretation of the Second Paragraph of Article 93 of the Criminal Code", *Legal Daily*, May 28, 2000.

special committee for reviewing and expressing an opinion." The above provisions incorporate the judicial interpretations made by the Supreme People's Court and the Supreme People's Procuratorate into the scope of the unified review conducted by the people's congress. These provisions make the decision about the conflict of laws among different rule makers clear, and unify the system of legal rules, resolve differences and uphold the authority of the law.

5.5 The Filing Review System as the Optimization Mechanism for the Legal System

On June 27, 2009, Wu Bangguo, Chairman of the Standing Committee of the National People's Congress, stressed: "The socialist legal system with Chinese characteristics will take shape by 2010 and will be continuously improved." In 2010, Chairman Wu Bangguo announced: "The socialist legal system has taken shape." As of the end of August, 2011, China had enacted 240 valid laws, covering seven legal branches including the Constitution and the constitution-related laws, civil and commercial law, administrative law, economic law, social law, criminal law, litigation and non-litigation procedural law, and 706 administrative regulations as well as more than 8,600 local regulations; a complete range of legal branches involving various aspects of social relationships had been covered; the basic, main laws in various legal branches had been made; the corresponding administrative regulations and local regulations were relatively complete; in general, the legal system was internally scientific, harmonious and unified; the socialist legal system with Chinese characteristics had taken shape. This was an important milestone in the construction of China's legal system.

Overall, after many years of building up China's legal system, it has become relatively complete. However, according to the theory of legal sociology, the laws in text or legal provisions are different from the laws in practice. As a Chinese saying goes, laws and decrees cannot come into force by themselves. At present, although China's legal system is relatively complete in form, many problems still exist in law enforcement. In realty, many legal norms are artificially crippled and become impracticable for many reasons. In fact, these crippled rules have negative effects on the rights of citizens. First, these crippled rules will disturb the rational expectations of citizens about laws. Second, they may bring about selective or random law enforcement.

Why do the above problems occur in law enforcement? Why do some laws lack actual effect? This is partly attributable to the problems in law enforcement, and partly due to the problems in the quality of legislation; for example, there are contradictions within the legal system; the laws at higher levels contradict the laws at lower levels and at the same level. Furthermore, some laws are abstractly expressed with political language and become inoperable. Some local legislative organs equate legislation with the drafting of political documents; as a result, the operability of part of the legal norms further decreases.

Against the background of a time in which the socialist legal system has taken shape, the days when there is a "legislative centralism" with lawmaking as its main task will soon disappear. The construction of the legal system focusing on legislation will disappear. In the new period, law enforcement will be especially emphasized and valued in the building up of China's legal system. As mentioned above, the effectiveness of laws cannot be guaranteed to some extent in law enforcement. The line of thought behind solving the problems in the quality of legislation should shift to legislation: first, the quality of legislation should be improved; for example, the democracy and scientificity of legislation should be strengthened. The resistance to scientific and democratic legislation in realty is mainly due to departmental interests in the departmental legislation; for example, some Chinese scholars believe that China's *Environmental Protection Law* has been crippled by other departmental legislations, thus becoming ineffective. For departmental interests, some people think that public interests are shared by departments, while departmental interests are controlled by groups. How can the above problems and drawbacks be overcome? Some scholars believe that it is necessary to reform the existing legislation procedure by incorporating more interest appeals into legislative discussions, especially the discussion process regarding the drafting of laws.

Will everything go smoothly after legislation becomes democratic? No. This is because the democratic process cannot guarantee the rule of good law. Some Chinese scholars believe that legislative corruption has surfaced in China; for example, the case of Zhou Jingyi involves legislative corruption. Some interest groups launch a lot of hype through media. Various kinds of legislative lobbies also affect the legislative process. As these lobbies develop and spread, the legitimacy and rationality of the legal system will certainly be affected. Therefore, it is necessary to supervise and control the legislative process. One of the effective solutions is that a channel should be provided beyond the legislative process for changing legal defects. This channel is the constitutional review of laws and regulations; in particular, the citizens and legal persons whose basic rights are subject to unjust legal infringement should be provided with the last relief approach according to the norms of basic rights prescribed by the Constitution. Such a system or mechanism would be of great significance to the building up of China's legal system. At present, there are many destabilizing factors in Chinese society, where some extreme violent incidents have occurred and some individuals resent the government. Once just appeals cannot be realized, some people will resort to extreme means. Some Chinese law scholars believe that a "pressure release valve" is still unavailable in the current legal system from the perspective of institutional design, while constitutional review provides the function of a "pressure release valve" — as the last relief mechanism, constitutional review might ensure that social appeals and contradictions are addressed within the legal system. Therefore, the Constitution serves as the fundamental basis for conducting constitutional review and control of the socialist legal system; thus on the one hand, the conflicts and mutual contradictions within the legal system could be removed; on the other hand, a legal channel could be provided for basic rights relief, and the legal mechanism for the guarantee of rights could be ameliorated, further improving the socialist legal system with Chinese characteristics.

With regard to the review system for China's laws and regulations, relevant regulations are not lacking at the level of legal norms; however, it is widely believed in the academic community that the effectiveness of review should be reinforced in China's current review system. First, the mechanism for clearing laws and regulations should be put in place on a regular basis so that problematic laws and regulations can be found, cleared and reviewed at any time without surprise clearing. If problems are discovered in specific cases, they should be opportunely delivered over to relevant organs for handling; for example, the handover procedure specified in the Legislation Law and Article 7 of the *Regulations for Citation of Normative Legal Documents Including Laws and Regulations in Judgment Documents*, as issued by the Supreme People's Court, is followed to deliver the problems found in specific cases to the organs of power for review at the opportune moment. Second, the existing filing review system should be implemented in an all-round way. It should not become formalistic, and the situation where filing is made but no review is conducted, and no conclusion is drawn, even if review is conducted, should be avoided. The appropriate opportunity and event should be chosen to initiate the constitutional review and practically safeguard the unity of the socialist legal system. Finally, attention should be paid to legislative inactions; the supporting legal provisions should be improved; the law and regulation system should become more perfect. There are many authorized legislation clauses in Chinese legal texts, such as "formulated by the State Council" and "formulated by relevant departments of the State Council"; however, many of these provisions do not materialize the supporting laws or regulations. In 2009, in the clearing procedure, the National People's Congress found that some laws explicitly prescribed that the supporting regulations should be made, but they had not yet been made; some laws did not have such explicit provision; there was a certain difficulty in law enforcement if no supporting regulations were available. Therefore, continuous improvement and optimization of the socialist legal system along with the enhancement of law enforcement represents a developmental trend for the construction of China's legal system.

Appendix Overview of Constitutional Supervision Systems in the Countries around the World[①]

I. Emergence and Development of Constitutional Supervision in the World

As an important constitutional system for guaranteeing the implementation of the constitution, the system of constitutional supervision has emerged and developed in a process basically the same as the process of the emergence and development of the constitution. However, the activity of constitutional supervision is, to some extent, independent from the implementation of the constitution, thus the system of constitutional supervision has its own characteristics in its emergence and development. So far, the system of constitutional supervision in the world has undergone several stages including exploration, development and maturity.

(I) The Stage of Exploration

The most striking practice of the system of constitutional supervision dates back to the constitutional supervision exercised by the Supreme

① Mo Jihong, "Theory and Practice of Constitutional Review", Law Press China, 2006.

Court of the United States in 1803.

According to the United States Constitution of 1787, the Federal Constitution does not specially authorize the Supreme Court of the United States to deal with the disputes relating to the Constitution, but the language of the Constitution provides sufficient evidence concerning such power. John Marshall, a chief justice of the Supreme Court of the United States, became the first to use the judicial review power to object to the congressional legislation in 1803 when he made a famous judgment — Marbury v. Madison case.① This judgment was made in the following historical conditions.

In the presidential election of 1800, the Federalists were defeated, but before leaving office, they appointed a number of new judges, including 42 Federalist judges appointed by the outgoing Federalist President John Adams from the District of Columbia. However, John Marshall, the Secretary of State during John Adams's term of office, did not deliver all of the commissions. After the new President Thomas Jefferson took office, he ordered his Secretary of State James Madison not to issue the commissions to 17 judges, including William Marbury. William Marbury decided to file a suit according to Article 13 of the Judiciary Act of 1789, which reads: "The Supreme Court has the power to, within the authority granted by legal systems and practice, issue court writs to the personnel working in the United States — a writ is an order issued by a court to require an official with the legal responsibility to perform duties." William Marbury immediately lodged an appeal to the U.S. Supreme Court through his lawyer, requiring the chief justice to issue a writ to the Secretary of State James Madison, ordering him to issue the commissions. However, John Marshall, the spokesperson of the U.S. Supreme Court —who had became the chief justice of that Court at that time — believed that Article 13 of the Judiciary Act of 1789 contravened the 1st paragraph of Article 3 of the Federal Constitution because the Constitution restricted the first trial authority of the Supreme Court to the cases to which ambassadors, ministers, consuls and states were parties. William Marbury fell outside all of the above categories, thus the Supreme Court refused to accept the case.

---

① Marbury V.Madison 5 U.S.137(1803).

Where did the U.S. Supreme Court's power to negate congressional legislation come from? John Marshall gave the following reason: the Constitution was a law, and a court was responsible for interpreting laws in order to decide a case according to the laws. The U.S. Supreme Court had the power to, and was also duty-bound to, interpret the Constitution; of course, its interpretation was in favor of the Constitution, rather than other laws. He also pointed out that the law which the Constitution authorized a court to enforce was the "highest law" from the perspectives of both the Congress and the Constitution (the 2nd paragraph of Article 6 of the Constitution). Herewith, before a law was enforced as "the highest law of the country", the U. S. Supreme Court had to first determine whether or not it complied with the Constitution.

Since then, the system of constitutional supervision based on the constitutional review system has developed rapidly, and reviewing whether or not laws, regulations and some important state acts comply with the Constitution to interpret the Constitution and guarantee the implementation of the constitution has become an important way to give play to the roles of the Constitution.

Since 1803, the Supreme Court of the United States has never questioned its power of constitutional review. The power of constitutional review has continued to work. The United States Supreme Court also has the power of constitutional review to determine whether or not state laws violate the Federal Constitution. The power of constitutional review was used 20 times during the American Civil War and the times were affected by it. Thirty-five state laws or presidential orders were declared unconstitutional from 1890 to 1932. In the initial period of the New Deal, from 1933 to 1935, the power to conduct constitutional review of laws was frequently used, and 12 laws were declared unconstitutional. President Franklin D. Roosevelt appointed judges who favored the New Deal, thus the U. S. Supreme Court exercised its power of constitutional review less. The U. S. Supreme Court took the judicial restraint attitude until 1945. As from 1953, the U. S. Supreme Court entered the era of the Warren Court, and became active in constitutional review. In the subsequent era of the Burger Court, the U. S. Supreme Court gradually became conservative towards constitutional review. However, the United States Supreme Court has never stopped safeguarding the authority of the Constitution. A judge from the U. S. Supreme Court said: "We are under the Constitution; however, what is called the Constitution is the law called the Constitution by judges."①

Guaranteeing the implementation of the constitution by the Supreme Court of the United States through constitutional review in more than 200 years has exerted a huge impact. So far, the Supreme Court of the United States has reviewed about 4,000 cases relating to constitutional interpretation, and has declared more than 80 laws made by the U.S. Congress unconstitutional. The number of state laws declared unconstitutional is larger. As the defender of the U.S. Constitution, the U.S. Supreme Court has made remarkable contributions to keeping the Constitution basically unchanged in more than 200 years since its promulgation. The U. S. Supreme Court is not the court dedicated to constitutional review; however, it has always dealt with the disputes possibly relating to the Constitution. The Constitution is always upheld in the U.S. political system and is a living constitution.

A number of written constitutions have been established in Continental Europe, but constitutional protection bodies with well-defined responsibilities have never existed, let alone a constitutional review body.

Shortly after the Bourgeois Revolution in France, some people proposed establishing a system of constitutional supervision, for which the representative figure was Sieyès, a famous French politician at the time. He suggested that a constitution committee (jurie constitutionnaire) should be set up to supervise the implementation of the constitution, put forward a draft amendment to it, and a judicial committee should be organized under the principle of natural equity in order to decide the cases which could not be tried by judges for the reason of conscience.② This suggestion was objected to. Afterwards, the parliament was very disgusted with such a motion; they believed that this supervision would lead to a "Government by Judges". However, in practice, the Constitution-protecting Senatus was established according to the 1799

① Li Yan, "Constitutional Review and Guarantee of Human Rights in Modern Countries", *Constitutionalism Review*, Vol.1, Law Press China, 1998, p.185.

② Zhu Guobin, "France's Constitutional Supervision and Constitutional Litigation System", *Journal of Comparative Law*, 1996 (3).

Constitution and the 1852 Constitution in France.

Germany experienced the Deutsch Alliance, Norddeutsche Alliance and Bismarck constitution era from 1815 to 1918. However, common courts had no power of law review during this period of more than 100 years. In the period of the Weimar Republic, according to the 2nd paragraph of Article 13 of the Weimar Constitution, the supreme federal official institution or the supreme official institution of a state having jurisdiction over the disputes on whether or not state laws contravened federal laws could apply to the State Affairs Court for making judgment. The State Affairs Court was established according to Article 108 of the Weimar Constitution and the *State Affairs Court Law of 1920.* However, the State Affairs Court mainly had jurisdiction over the cases of non-private-law disputes among states and between the federation and the states, and had no jurisdiction over whether or not federal laws contravened the Weimar Constitution. Therefore, the State Affairs Court did not function as a constitutional court during that period. What really granted the State Affairs Court the power of constitutional review was the judgment made by the Fifth Civil Adjudication Tribunal of the Supreme Federal Court on November 4, 1925. This judgment held that Article 102 of the Weimar Constitution had affirmed the principle, prescribed by Article 1 of the *Court Organization Law*, that judges were independent and only amenable to laws; however, where the federal laws applied by judges contravened the Weimar Constitution, or state laws contravened federal laws, such principles did not preclude the power of judges not to recognize the validity of these laws and not to apply them. Judges should be considered as having the power to determine whether or not federal laws complied with the Constitution. This judgment officially established the role of the German State Affairs Court in upholding the authority of the Constitution. However, such a role only lasted for a very short time during wartime, and disappeared as the Weimar Constitution was discarded by the Nazi régime.①

Austria was the first country to establish a constitutional court. It instituted a constitutional court for guaranteeing the implementation of

① Liu Zhaoxing, "Abstract Review Power of the German Federal Constitutional Court", *Constitutionalism Review*, Vol.1, Law Press China, 1998, pp.209-2011.

the constitution in Continental Europe in 1920. Moreover, the Czech Republic and Spain also established a similar constitutional review body. Such constitutional courts based constitutional review on specific rights and obligation disputes, and once a certain law was declared by such a constitutional court as unconstitutional, that law lost legal validity. The Constitutional Court of Austria consisted of special judges with life tenure; when these judges suspected that any applicable law or order was unconstitutional, they would review that law; where a common court suspected, when deciding a case, that the order applied by it was unlawful, it should suspend its trial, and request the Constitutional Court to annul this order. Therefore, the Constitutional Court of Austria was higher than any common court and enjoyed very great power; it had the power to review all laws and orders suspected of contravening the constitution.

The Czech Constitutional Court, established after the First World War, divided constitutional violations by laws into constitutional violations in form and constitutional violations in substance. The constitutional violations in form were reviewed by the common court — the common court had the power to review the legal form, such as reviewing whether a certain law was promulgated according to laws and whether the legislative procedure complied with the constitution. The constitutional violations in substance were reviewed by the Constitutional Court — the Constitutional Court had the power to review whether the contents of laws complied with the constitution, in other words, the Constitutional Court had the power to review whether the contents of laws contravened the constitution, but the contents of orders were reviewed by the common court. Therefore, the Czech Constitutional Court was not higher than the common courts and coexisted with the common courts to share the power of constitutional review; thus legally, the scope of the power of constitutional supervision of the Czech Constitutional Court was narrower than that of the power of constitutional supervision enjoyed by the Constitutional Court of Austria.[1]

---

① Mo Jihong, "New Constitutional Theory", China Fangzheng Press, 1997, pp.114-115.

(II) The Stage of the Development

After the Second World War, given that the Nazi régime had trampled on the constitution and human rights during the Second World War, many countries shifted their attention to how to guarantee the implementation of the constitution. In such a circumstance, in the countries with the common law tradition, the Supreme Court had the power to review whether laws complied with the constitution; for example, the Federal Court of Switzerland and the Supreme Court in Nordic countries[①] had the power to review whether or not laws, regulations and important constitutional acts complied with the constitution. In the countries with the continental law tradition, some special bodies dedicated to guaranteeing the implementation of the constitution were established — some were special judicial organs and some were constitutional supervision bodies; for example, France established the Constitution Committee in 1946 and changed it to the Constitutional Court (or it was still called the Constitution Committee) during the period of the Fifth Republic.[②] Italy established the Constitutional Court in 1947. Germany established the Constitutional Court in 1949.

Two qualitative changes took place in the practice of constitutional supervision after the Second World War. First, the Supreme Court in many common law countries emulated the constitutional review system of the Supreme Court of the United States to establish a system for guaranteeing the implementation of the constitution by means of judicial adjudication. Second, some countries established a special

---

① Both the Supreme Court and the Supreme Administrative Court in Finland and Sweden enjoyed the judicial power.

② The Constitution Committee established during the period of the French Fourth Republic and that during the period of the Fifth Republic were expressed in the French comité constitutionnel and conseil constitutionnel respectively; however, the Constitution Committee during the period of the Fifth Republic could accept litigation, so it was also called the Constitutional Court to differentiate from the Constitution Committee during the period of the Fourth Republic. In fact, the special issues of the *Constitutional Case Law Communiqué* edited by the Venice Commission of the Council of Europe often translated conseil constitutionnel and conseil constitutionnel into constitutional court and constitution committee respectively, both were interchangeable.

constitutional court to deal with constitutional cases, and thanks to such an establishment, the scope of constitutional review was expanded and the role of constitutional review became increasingly prominent.

For example, the Constitutional Court of Federal Germany came into play as of 1951 and it had heard 41,127 constitutional cases and dealt with 39,920 constitutional cases by 1978. These cases included 38,789 constitutional litigation cases, 1,795 abstract review cases, 2 cases involving constitutional violation by political parties and 541 other cases.[①] The Constitution Committee of the French Fifth Republic was less active in conducting constitutional review activities at the initial stage. Since 1971, the Constitution Committee has established the legal validity of the preamble to France's Constitution, and reviewed that preamble as a whole; it affirmed the freedom of association as the basic principle for various laws of the Republic, so the development of the constitutional review system was promoted and many famous constitutional review cases occurred, such as the case involving infringement of foreigners' personal freedom on January 9, 1980; the case involving constitutional violation of the law which provided that females should account for 25% of those elected on November 28, 1982; the case involving the interruption of pregnancy on January 15, 1975; the case involving decentralization on February 25, 1982; the case involving the nationalization act on January 16, 1982, etc. According to statistics, the Constitution Committee reviewed 46 organizational laws and rejected 4 of them, from 1958 when the Constitution Committee was established, to 1986 — the reasons for such rejection included: causing damage to the principle, designed to guarantee judicial independence, that judges were irremovable; treating the contents which can be used for organizing laws as parliamentary rules; violating the constitutional provision that a parliamentarian cannot concurrently hold an inappropriate position. The rules of the House and the Senate were submitted by relevant speakers to the Constitution Committee for review after they were passed. According to statistics, the Constitution Committee made 33 decisions concerning parliamentary rules from 1958, when the Constitution Committee was

① Zhang Qingfu (ed.), "Constitutionalism Review", Vol.1, Law Press China, 1998, p.190.

established, to 1986.[①]

The countries where the "incidental" constitutional review system was adopted after the Second World War were less active in the practical activities of constitutional review than the countries where a constitutional court had been established; for example, in Japan, the Supreme Court exercised the power of constitutional review only five times before the 1980s, showing a very obvious passivism in constitutional review, while there were fewer cases in which the Supreme Court ruled that there were constitutional violations. The Supreme Court of Japan was passive in constitutional review compared with the system of constitutional review in the U.S.A., France and Germany; this was criticized by Japanese constitutional scholars.

(III) The Stage of Maturity

The roles of the system of constitutional supervision have been fully reflected through the practical activities of constitutional review in various countries since the late 1980s, revealing the following several obvious characteristics:

First, after the upheaval, the Soviet Union, Central and Eastern European countries established constitutional courts and granted them with relatively large powers, so a number of new constitutional courts accepted and heard a very large number of constitutional cases, mainly because the people generally considered the constitutional courts as the defenders of the constitution and anchored their expectations about guaranteeing the rights and powers prescribed by the constitution on constitutional courts; for example, the Constitutional Court of Hungary came into play on January 1, 1990, and afterwards, it accepted and heard more than 1,700 cases on average each year; it accepted and heard 735 cases in 1990, and entered judgments, about 2/3 of them in 1990, handled 195, 20 and 16 cases in 1991, 1992 and 1993, respectively. It accepted 6,950 cases and heard 2,356 cases (the cases heard were about 34% of the cases accepted), entered judgments, about 1,939 cases (82%

① Zhang Qingfu (ed.), "Constitutionalism Review", Vol.1, Law Press China, 1998, p.257.

of the cases heard) in these four years.[①] The dramatically increasing number of constitutional cases strained the judgment capability of the constitutional courts.

Second, some long-standing constitutional courts handled a raft of constitutional violation cases in their long-term practice of constitutional review, thus various legal contradictions were resolved better; the number of constitutional cases from state organs was relatively small, while constitutional litigations lodged by citizens made up a considerably large proportion of the cases of constitutional review, so the constitution really protected the basic rights of citizens; for example, in Federal Germany, the adjudication tribunals under the Federal Constitutional Court heard cases and entered 9 judgments — all of the judgments were related to the constitutional litigations lodged by citizens — and conducted joint trials of 4 cases from September 1, 1996 to December 31, 1996. The adjudication tribunals under the Federal Constitutional Court heard cases and entered 6 judgments — all of the judgments involved constitutional litigations lodged by citizens — and conducted a joint trial of 1 case from January 1, 1997 to April 30, 1997. The adjudication tribunals under the Federal Constitutional Court heard cases and entered 5 judgments — all of the judgments involved constitutional litigations lodged by citizens — and conducted a joint trial of 1 case from May 1, 1997 to August 31, 1997.[②] As shown, all the cases handled by the Federal Constitutional Court of Germany in the whole year from September 1, 1996 to August 31, 1997 were cases involving constitutional litigations lodged by citizens, and the roles of citizens in supervising unconstitutional laws and addressing constitutional violations in modern democratic society became more and more important.

Third, the European countries have been cooperating with each other in constitutional review. Such cooperation is reflected in the following two aspects: On the one hand, experience and communication in constitutional review is enhanced among the constitutional courts in various countries through the Conference on European Constitutional

① Zhang Qingfu, "Constitutionalism Review", Vol.1, Law Press China, 1998, p.205.

② the *"Constitutional Case Law Communiqué"* edited by the Venice Commission of the Council of Europe, 1995 (2), 1996 (1-3) and 1997 (1-3).

Courts; on the other hand, as the European Court of Human Rights and the European Court of Justice have the judicial adjudication power beyond the constitutional courts of various member states, the member states of the Council of Europe and EU member states have to reach a consensus on the basic constitutional issues to support the decision being generally binding upon all member states as made by the European Court of Human Rights and the European Court of Justice; as a result, constitutional review becomes an indispensable system. The constitutions within states serve as the intermediary among the EU laws, *the European Convention on Human Rights* and the laws within relevant member states. The relationship among the legal systems of member states, the EU legal system and the legal system of the Council of Europe cannot be rationalized without the roles of constitutions; therefore, the system of constitutional review becomes the primary judicial adjudication system.

After the Second World War, the system of constitutional review gradually became mature, while the most noteworthy phenomenon in this process was the popularization of the mode of the constitutional court. After the upheaval in the Soviet Union, most Central and Eastern European countries from 1989 to 1991, established the constitutional courts, marking the rule of law. After the establishment of the constitutional courts, these countries actively attended the Conference on European Constitutional Courts consisting of the traditional countries where the system of constitutional review was adopted. The Conference on European Constitutional Courts was convened in Paris, France in 1992, with the participation of many representatives from Central and Eastern European countries. The Conference on the Constitutional Courts of Central and Eastern European Countries was held in Warsaw, Poland in 1994, where most of the countries provided reports. However, several of them did not adopt the mode of the constitutional court; instead, they made reference to the U.S. system of constitutional review — a special body is established under the U. S. Supreme Court to hear constitution-related cases. The most typical country was Estonia, where a constitutional review court was established under the Supreme Court to hear constitutional cases.

When establishing the constitutional courts, these countries often developed specific legal rules for the constitutional courts to conduct activities regarding constitutional review; these rules are divided into two categories: first, affirming the status of the constitutional court in the constitution, and specifying the basic functions of the constitutional court; second, developing a special constitutional court organization and procedural laws to institutionalize and standardize trials in the constitutional court; for example, Chapter Two of the *Constitution of the Republic of Albania,* passed on April 29, 1992, details the functions and powers of the constitutional court; Chapter Eight of the *Constitution of the Republic of Bulgaria,* passed on July 12, 1991, provides for the constitutional court, the *Law of the Constitutional Court* was passed according to the Constitution on July 30, 1991; Chapter Five of the *Constitution of the Republic of Croatia,* passed on December 22, 1990, prescribes the functions and powers of the constitutional court, the *Constitutional Law of the Republic of Croatia on the Constitutional Court* was passed on March 21, 1991; the Czech Republic passed the *Constitutional Court Law* on June 16, 1993; Estonia passed the *Procedural Law on the Constitutional Review Tribunal*; Hungary enacted the *No.32 Law of the Constitutional Court of 1989* and revised it in 1994; Latvia passed the *Constitutional Court Law* on June 5, 1996; Lithuania passed the *Constitutional Court Law of Lithuania* on February 3, 1993 and revised it in on July 11, 1996; Poland made the *Constitutional Court Law* on April 29, 1985; the No.47 Law of 1992, in Romania on May 18, 1992 is the *Law on Constitutional Court Organization and Activity*; Chapter One of the 7th Section "Judicial Power" of the *Constitution of the Slovak Republic*, passed in the Slovak Republic on September 3, 1992, prescribes the functions and powers of the constitutional court; the National Assembly of the Slovak Republic passed the *Law of the Slovak Republic on the Organization of the Constitutional Court, Litigations of the Constitutional Court and the Status of the Constitutional Court Judges* on January 20, 1993; Slovenia's *Constitution of 1991* provides for the legal status of the constitutional court; the *Constitutional Court Law* was enacted in 1994. According to the survey conducted by the Venice Commission of the Council of Europe, all countries, as its members, relational members or observers have established a system of constitutional review; the organizational forms of the system of constitutional review are mainly divided into two categories.

The first category refers to the special constitutional review body, involving such countries as Albania, Armenia, Azerbaijan, Belgium, the Republic of Bosnia and Herzegovina, Bulgaria, Croatia, the Czech Republic, France, Georgia, Germany, Hungary, Italy, Latvia, Liechtenstein, Lithuania, Poland, Portugal, Romania, Russia, Slovenia, Slovakia, Spain, Turkey and Ukraine.

Another category involves the exercise of the power of constitutional review by common courts, mainly the Supreme Court. The countries where the Supreme Court exercises the constitutional court power include Argentina, Canada, Cyprus, Demark, Estonia, Greece, Iceland, Ireland, Japan, Malta, Norway, Sweden and Switzerland.

In addition, besides the members of the Conference on European Constitutional Courts, many countries also have established a system of constitutional review, such as South Korea and South Africa.

Since the Second World War, the issue of human rights has become a common issue for the international community, and protection of human rights has exceeded the scope of the traditional national countries. Therefore, the international or regional human rights courts which enjoy the judicial adjudication power over the matters concerning the protection of human rights beyond national countries have come into being. In terms of legal force, these courts do not have ex officio jurisdiction over all countries, and only the countries which recognize their jurisdiction are bound by these courts. The characteristic of these international courts is that they accept and hear the cases for which relief approaches have been exhausted in domestic courts, and the plaintiffs may be countries or citizens. At present, these courts mainly include the International Court of Justice, the European Court of Human Rights, the Inter-American Court of Human Rights and the European Court of Justice. From the perspective of legal functions, these courts actually act as the constitutional courts at another level. This is because the cases heard by these courts are often the cases heard by the constitutional courts in the countries where the cases are involved or the courts exercising the power of constitutional review in these countries; furthermore, the results of case hearings are accepted by the contracting parties, thus these international human rights courts are the constitutional courts which exercise the adjudication power to protect the human rights prescribed by the constitutions of the contracting parties outside the national countries — this nature arises from the international protection of human rights; if a contracting party which recognizes that an international human rights court has jurisdiction over it believes that the judicial jurisdiction over it enjoyed by the international human rights courts is detrimental to its sovereignty or there are other reasons, this country may make a statement to withdraw such commitment at any time; this principle is explicitly stipulated in many international conventions on human rights, such as the *European Convention on Human Rights*; thus the international human rights courts cannot become operative unless the roles of the international human rights courts, outside of the national countries, as the constitutional courts must be based on the *Vienna Convention on the Law of Treaties*;[①] this is the fundamental difference between the international human rights courts and the constitutional courts exercising the power of constitutional review in national countries.

Overall, the roles of the system of constitutional supervision have drawn increasing attention from the modern democratic and law-ruled countries. As the constitution has become the operable law in practice, the roles of the constitution as the fundamental law of a state have been increasingly found in the modern democratic system and every part of the rule of law. The modern constitutional system with the constitution as the core has become the most important feature of modern democracy and rule of law.

① Article 19 of the *Vienna Convention on the Law of Treaties* reads, "a State may, when signing, ratifying, accepting, approving or acceding to a treaty, formulate a reservation unless: (a) the reservation is prohibited by the treaty; (b) the treaty provides that only specified reservations, which do not include the reservation in question, may be made; or (c) in cases not falling under sub-paragraphs (a) and (b), the reservation is incompatible with the object and purpose of the treaty. " According to this article, the force of an international treaty on a national country should be legally understood as a legal force equivalent to domestic laws. The difference is that domestic laws only have the legal force on one country, while the international laws have the legal force on many countries; however, the legal force of the international laws on many countries is unequal to that of domestic laws, and must be considered in the light of the characteristics of the legal force of domestic laws.

II. Main Categories of Constitutional Supervision in the World

At present, the constitutional supervision systems in countries around the world mainly focus on the review of the legal documents formulated by the legislative bodies, and different types of constitutional supervisory modes under which special constitutional review bodies conduct a constitutional review of laws have taken shape in the practice of constitutional supervision — the main characteristic of the system of constitutional review.

The judicial review of laws by special constitutional courts or special constitutional review bodies for constitutional compliance is divided into two main types:

(1) Review beforehand — laws are reviewed before they are passed; for example, there are provisions in this regard in the 1st paragraph and the 2nd paragraph of Article 61 of France's Constitution and its Article 41; the 2nd paragraph of Article 138 of Austria's Constitution "Review of the Legislation Capacity of the Federation or State"; the 4th paragraph of Article 127 of Italy's Constitution "Provision Concerning Affirmation of Whether the Legislative Authority is Infringed"; the 1st, 2nd and 4th paragraphs of Article 278 of Portugal's Constitution; Article 26 of Ireland's Constitution, etc.

(2) Post review — the laws which have been passed are reviewed for constitutional compliance.

(I) Review Beforehand

Review beforehand often requires the constitutional courts to answer relevant questions within the specified time so that laws can be opportunely passed, thus compared with post review, the review time will not be delayed and it is also easy to prevent the introduction of obviously unconstitutional low-level laws. It can enhance the authority of lawmakers, especially in the case where constitutional violations by laws are found in post review; it can ensure that the force disputes concerning international laws are settled before the law which ratifies international treaties is passed.

Review beforehand also has some disadvantages compared with

post review; for example, it demands immediate answer to questions concerning relatively complicated political, economic and legal issues in a very short time, while the significance of many laws only lies in "the law in action", and so review beforehand might fail to discover the constitutional violations by these laws during enforcement. As there are no specific examples that can serve as reference, the abstract review which only touches upon the surface often overlooks the substantive issues. With changing social and economic conditions, it is very easy to cause constitutional violations by "the law in action"; however, such problems cannot be effectively supervised at the judicial level after the law is passed. Review beforehand also easily hinders legislation from better reflecting the actual requirements of the society. Therefore, compared with review beforehand, post review appears to more effectively give play to the role of judicature in constitutional supervision over laws. Of course, review beforehand is relatively beneficial to the ratified laws regarding international treaties.

One of the solutions to the above problems is the combination of review beforehand and post review; for example, an inferior court is permitted to lodge an appeal to the constitutional court when it finds, upon hearing a case, that the laws applied contravene the constitution, or citizens are permitted to file a constitutional litigation concerning an unconstitutional court decision to the constitutional court — such as Article 280 of Portugal's Constitution and Article 69 of Portugal's *Constitutional Court Law*—, or request an abstract constitutional review — Article 281 of Portugal's Constitution and Article 62 of Portugal's *Constitutional Court Law*. However, a combination of both review modes is very likely to affect the stability of the laws (rechtssicherheit); in particular, the laws considered as consistent with the constitution by a court in review beforehand are found to contravene the constitution in post review, in which case, it is very likely to affect the authority of the judicial review of laws for constitutional compliance. However, such a combination is relatively feasible if there is a certain difference — review beforehand focuses on the disputes concerning the legislative authority, while post review centers on substantive constitutional violations by the laws under review. However, in a federal country, it is not easy to make an explicit decision on the legislative authority of the relevant federation or state in a very short time.

Although there are debates like the ones above on the advantages and disadvantages of the system of review beforehand, in countries where the system of review beforehand is adopted, the laws involving the ratification of international treaties are delivered to the constitutional court for review beforehand; many procedural issues concerning delivery of other laws to the constitutional court for review beforehand also deserve to be further studied and investigated; the main issues are shown below:

First, what is the most appropriate time for initiating the procedure for review beforehand — whether to conduct review before or after the final vote by the legislative body (for the former, such as Article 41 of France's Constitution; for the latter, such as the 1st and 2nd paragraphs of Article 61 of France's Constitution). Before the legislative body finally votes on the law under review, the law is reviewed for constitutional compliance; if constitutional violations are found, the legislative body can be urged to further revise and improve a draft law so that it is not declared as unconstitutional by the constitutional court.

Second, whoever has the power to trigger this procedure of review beforehand — compulsory, such as the 1st paragraph of Article 61 of France's Constitution; voluntary, such as the 2nd paragraph of Article 61 of France's Constitution, the 1st, 2nd and 4th paragraphs of Article 278 of Portugal's Constitution, the 1st paragraph of Article 26 of Ireland's Constitution. Compulsory submission for review can provide an authoritative exemption basis for delayed legislation, and can ensure that the law which has undergone review beforehand is not subject to dispute again in terms of constitutional compliance.

Third, the issue of time limit — this issue covers two aspects: first, the time limit for submission for review, which is generally very short so that legislation is not subject to delay; the 3rd paragraph of Article 278 of Portugal's Constitution provides that it is 8 days, while the 1st paragraph of Article 26 of Ireland's Constitution stipulates that it does not exceed 7 days. Second, the time limit for conducting review and making a decision, which is also restricted as much as possible; the 3rd paragraph of Article 61 and the 3rd paragraph of Article 41 of France's Constitution provide that it is one month;, and at the government's request, it may be shortened to 8 days in case of emergency; the 8th paragraph of Article 278 of Portugal's Constitution stipulates that it is 25 days, and the President of the Republic may shorten this time limit; the 1st subparagraph of the 2nd paragraph of Article 26 of Ireland's Constitution provides that it must not exceed 20 days.

Generally, the draft laws which should be delivered for constitutional review include all laws, such as the 2nd paragraph of Article 61 of France's Constitution, the 1st paragraph of Article 278 of Portugal's Constitution; special laws, such as the 1st paragraph of Article 61 of France's Constitution; the laws which ratify the international treaties, such as the 1st paragraph of Article 278 of Portugal's Constitution. Review beforehand of the laws which ratify the international treaties can effectively prevent relevant international treaties from failing to exert the force of international law on the country concerned due to noncompliance with the domestic legal system; this merit is the most important factor contributing to the adoption of the system of review beforehand. In some countries, review beforehand is excluded for some special laws — such as the 1st paragraph of Article 26 of Ireland's Constitution — these laws generally include amendments to the constitution, the laws for referendum and laws of the state of emergency. In some countries, the legal norms which are one level lower than laws are delivered to the constitutional court for review beforehand; for example, the 2nd paragraph of Article 278 of Portugal's Constitution states that regional regulations and the regulations for implementing general laws should, when enacted, be delivered to the constitutional court for review beforehand.

The scope of review beforehand: only reviewing whether the legislation procedure prescribed by the constitution is complied with; the issue of the legislative authority. If the laws under review beforehand are reviewed for constitutional compliance of the legislative authority and procedure of the lawmaking body and the substantive content of the laws under review is also reviewed — such as whether there is compliance with the basic rights, freedom, standards and principles prescribed by the constitution, such a general review mode will certainly cause various problems due to the lack of necessary practical experience. However, unrestricted review beforehand of the laws which ratify the international treaties may avoid constitutional violations to the greatest extent. Therefore, if review beforehand focuses on the legislative procedure and the legislative authority for constitutional compliance, a very large space can be reserved for post review.

The application for initiating review beforehand may suspend the legislative procedure; for example, laws should not be promulgated (the 4th paragraph of Article 61 of France's Constitution, the 1st paragraph of Article 26 of Ireland's Constitution); this often impedes legislation but can prevent unconstitutional laws from being introduced and executed. Where the constitutional court finds that the law under review contravenes the constitution and makes a decision, the promulgation of this law can be prevented; where the constitutional court does not find constitutional violations, the law should be promptly promulgated and brought into force. However, this reviewing act can be overturned by the result of special voting by the legislative body; for example, the 2nd and 4th paragraphs of Article 279 of Portugal's Constitution state that 2/3 of the members of parliament can veto the decision made by the constitutional court with respect to international treaties; the 4th paragraph of Article 27 and the 2nd paragraph of Article 33 of Poland's Constitution and the 3rd and 4th paragraphs of Article 6 of the *Constitutional Court Law* of Poland also contain the same provision. The law which is found to contravene the constitution should be delivered by the constitutional court to the parliament so that the law can be changed to ensure that it complies with the constitution; for example, the 1st paragraph of Article 279 of Portugal's Constitution, the 2nd paragraph of Article 33 and the 2nd paragraph of Article 35 of the No.32 Law of Hungary of 1989 incorporate such a provision, and the parliament can also veto the decision made by the constitutional court, depending upon the status and role of the parliament. For the force of the decision made by the constitutional court, a view holds that the decision made by the constitutional court, which shows that a law under review contravenes the constitution, can deny a law made by the parliament in the future if it is the same as the law which contravenes the constitution; such a view is very likely to incur a question: Whether the contents of both laws are the same.

(II) Post Review

The main issues relating to the system of post review include: (1) which kind of laws should be reviewed; (2) who can file a review application and in what capacity he or she acts; (3) whether a review is conducted by a disputed procedure or an objective procedure (no answers for the plaintiff); (4) which bodies or individuals, except the plaintiff, have the power to participate in litigation or have the opportunity to be questioned by the court; (5) to what extent the constitutional court should conduct a constitutional review of laws (whether a review only focuses on the alleged constitutional violations or whether a comprehensive review is conducted); (6) the contents and force of the decision made by the constitutional court.

In general, all types of laws in a country should be subject to post review, including laws, the rules of procedure of the parliament, decrees or regulations with legal force, laws of the federation, a region or community. A review of laws by the constitutional court is generally based on their importance, their statuses in the legal system of a country and the actual capability of the constitutional court for handling such kinds of issues. Generally, the laws to be reviewed by the constitutional court should be mainly those enacted by the parliament; this is because these laws cannot be annulled by the ordinary courts in normal conditions, while the laws at lower levels may be reviewed by the courts at relatively low levels. Besides the ordinary laws enacted by the parliament and to be reviewed by the constitutional court, the following laws may also be considered:

(1) The laws which revise the constitution. This is based on the following assumption: The parliament should be bound by the constitution and does not fully represent the sovereignty, and the constitution restricts the parliament in changing constitutional provisions. A review of the laws which revise the constitution means that the constitutional court is generally considered as "the defender of the constitution" against the parliament. A review mainly covers the capability of lawmakers or procedure; for example, the 1st paragraph of Article 148 of Turkey's Constitution of 1982 contains such a provision. The constitutional amendment must be consistent with the constitution

only in form, and the substantive contents of the laws under review should not be reviewed for constitutional compliance. However, in practice, there are also reviews of the substantive contents of the laws under review; for example, the 3rd paragraph of Article 79 of Germany's *Basic Law Concerning Revision of Some Principles in the Fundamental Law* contains such a provision. An extensive review of a constitutional amendment will also lead to the situation where some principles in the constitution cannot be revised unless they severely affect the basic spirit enshrined in the constitution. Accordingly, the constitution is kept unchanged by the State organ of power because actually any constitutional amendment must be based on a recommendation made by the State organ of power.

(2) The organizational laws or similar laws, such as the constitutional law — there is such a system in Austria— a review mainly covers the legislative capability, procedure and substantive content.

(3) The laws made through a referendum — a review mainly covers the legislative capability, procedure and substantive content.

(4) The laws which ratify international treaties — a review mainly covers the legislative capability, procedure and substantive contents. The laws which ratify international treaties are generally understood in such a manner that the State organ ensures that the international treaties have legal force in the country concerned and the international treaties should have the same legal force as domestic laws. However, if an international treaty has the same binding force as the international law, but the law which ratifies this international treaty is declared unconstitutional, conflicts arise. According to Article 27 of the *Vienna Convention on the Law of Treaties*, a party may not invoke the provisions of its internal law as justification for its failure to perform a treaty.

(5) The laws before the entry into force of the new constitution. This issue is extremely important for establishing the new constitution. The *German Fundamental Law of 1949* provides that all laws made before the entry into force of the fundamental law which contravene the fundamental law should cease to have effect. However, the constitutional review of these laws is not the privilege of the constitutional court; if a general court finds that these laws contravene the fundamental law when hearing a case, that court refuses to apply these laws though it has no

power to officially declare them invalid.

(6) State laws; for example, there is a special post review system for state laws in Switzerland.

(7) The possibility that some laws are subject to post review is precluded, such as laws and decrees of a state of emergency. The 1st paragraph of Article 148 of Turkey's Constitution contains such a provision. However, noteworthily, if laws of a state of emergency are not reviewed for constitutional compliance, it is very easy to infringe upon the legislative authority of the parliament.

(8) The laws at lower levels. If all laws at lower levels are reviewed by the constitutional court for constitutional compliance, the constitutional court will be overburdened due to a heavy review workload. Therefore, the ordinary courts review the laws at lower levels, and the highest court among the ordinary courts makes the final decision about the constitutional compliance of the laws at lower levels.

(9) The rules of procedure of the parliament, for example, Article 34 of the No.32 Law of Hungary of 1989 concerning the Constitutional Court contains such a provision.

Applying for initiating the post constitutional review procedure in an established constitutional system is very important. Comparatively, there are the following six categories of applicants for initiating the procedure of constitutional review:

(1) The highest organ of state power, such as the president of a republic, the head of state, the central government, the legislative organ, a certain number of members of the legislative organ, the prime minister, attorney general, parliament ombudsperson, federal or local state organs which claim that laws infringe the powers granted to them by the constitution. For example, Article 1 and Article 2 of Belgium's *Arbitration Court Law*, Article 37 and Article 39 of the No.87 Law of Italy of 1953, the 2nd paragraph of Article 140 of Austria's Constitution, the 2nd Paragraph of Article 281 of Portugal's Constitution, the 1st paragraph of Article 161 and the 2nd paragraph of Article 162 of Spain's Constitution, the 2nd subparagraph of the 1st paragraph of Article 93 of the *German Fundamental Law* contain the above provision. Noteworthily, in some countries, a small number of parliamentarians may also apply for initiating the post constitutional review; for example, in Portugal, such a

number is 1/10 of the parliamentarians in the parliament of the Republic. Article 150 of Turkey's Constitution and the 1st subparagraph of the 1st paragraph of Article 162 of Spain's Constitution also incorporate a similar provision; Austria's Constitution provides that 1/3 of the members of the National Assembly may apply for initiating the post constitutional review; in Federal Germany, 1/3 of the Bundestag's members may apply for initiating the post constitutional review; such provision ensures that the minority group in the parliament also has the power to make a request about constitutional review of laws to the constitutional court. The power to make a constitutional review request to the Federal Constitutional Court can also be exercised by the organs under the central government, states, and autonomous regions; for example, there is a similar provision in Belgium.

(2) The ordinary courts also have the power to make a post constitutional review request to the Constitutional Court. Generally, where an ordinary court finds, when hearing a case, that the laws on which the decision is based may contravene the constitution, it should make a constitutional review request to the constitutional court, and take the decision made by the constitutional court as the conclusive basis for judgment. As the case is specially heard by the constitutional court according to the constitutional review request made in such a way, this is conducive to preventing the situation where different courts enter different judgments based on the same legal provisions because they act in their own ways.

The constitutional review requests made by the ordinary courts to the constitutional court are diverse in category and circumstance; for example, the 1st subparagraph of the 1st paragraph of Article 140 of Austria's Constitution provides that the Supreme Administrative Court, the Supreme Court and the appellate court for the trial of second instance have the power to make a post review request to the constitutional court regarding the unconstitutional laws. Furthermore, Article 152 of Spain's Constitution, Article 26 of Belgium's *Arbitration Court Law* and the 1st paragraph of Article 100 of the *German Fundamental Law* contain the above provision.

(3) Where local and municipal bodies, which enjoy the power of self-government as prescribed by the constitution, believe that laws infringe

upon their power granted by the constitution, they may also make a constitutional review request to the constitutional court about these laws so as to guarantee such authorization from the constitution; for example, the 9th paragraph of Article 119 and Article 144 of Austria's Constitution, the 4th subparagraph of the 1st paragraph of Article 93 of the *German Fundamental Law o f 1949* contain such a provision.

(4) Where individuals or groups believe that laws infringe upon the basic rights and freedom they enjoy as prescribed by the constitution, they may also bring a constitutional litigation involving a constitutional review request to the constitutional court; for example, the 2nd subparagraph of the 1st paragraph of Article 161, the 2nd subparagraph of the 1st paragraph of Article 162 and the 2nd paragraph of Article 53 of Spain's Constitution, the 4th subparagraph of the 1st paragraph of Article 140 of Austria's Constitution, the 4th subparagraph of the 1st paragraph of Article 93 of the *German Fundamental Law* contain such a provision. Where personal rights are infringed upon by the acts of administrative organs or judicial organs due to laws, a special constitutional litigation mode may be adopted. In some countries, in order to prevent excessive constitutional litigations, there is a provision that individuals must lodge a constitutional litigation on the grounds that personal constitutional rights or freedom are or is directly infringed upon by relevant laws; for example, the 2nd and 4th paragraphs of Article 21 of the No.32 Law of Hungary of 1989 concerning the constitutional court contain such a provision. In some countries, laws make a distinction among different constitutional litigation modes: individuals or groups directly make a constitutional review request about the laws which infringe upon their constitutional rights, and individuals or groups lodge a constitutional litigation on the grounds that the laws on which the decision made by the administrative organs or judicial organs with respect to individuals or groups is based may contravene the constitution; for example, Article 280 of Portugal's Constitution and Article 144 of Austria's Constitution contain such a provision.

(5) The constitutions of some countries also provide that the public procuratorial office or parliament ombudsperson, as "the defender of the constitution", may make a constitutional review request regarding laws; for example, the 1st subparagraph of the 1st paragraph of Article 162 of

Spain's Constitution, the 1st and 2nd paragraphs of Article 19 of Poland's *Constitutional Court Law* incorporate such a provision.

(6) In some countries, the constitutional court itself may also review the unconstitutional laws; for example, the 3rd paragraph of Article 19 of Poland's *Constitutional Court Law* and the last paragraph of Article 387 of the Constitution of the Socialist Federal Republic of Yugoslavia contain such a provision, while such a provision appears to place more emphasis on the role of the constitutional court as the defender of the constitution.

This book is the result of a co-publication agreement between China Social Sciences Press (China) and Paths International Ltd (UK)

Report on Constitutional Enforcement and Constitutional Review in China
Authors: Li Lin, Zhai Guoqiang
ISBN: 978-1-84464-506-0
Ebook ISBN: 978-1-84464-507-7

Paths International Ltd
PO Box 4083
Reading
United Kingdom
RG8 8ZN
www.pathsinternational.com

Published in the United Kingdom

CPSIA information can be obtained
at www.ICGtesting.com
Printed in the USA
LVHW062038260220
648310LV00004B/5

9 781844 645060